PRAISE FOR
TURN THE TIDE

"This is an excellent resource! Kathy Obear brilliantly illuminates the anatomy of difficult situations and offers sage practical guidance to help employers and employees gain greater self-awareness and to better maneuver problems not only in the work place, but also for any frustrating interaction."

Sherry K. Watt, Ph. D.

Associate Professor, Higher Education and Student Affairs, University of Iowa, author and editor of *Designing Transformative Multicultural Initiatives: Theoretical Foundations, Practical Applications, and Facilitator Considerations*

"With compassion, clarity and wisdom, Kathy Obear offers page after page of helpful insights and strategies for navigating difficult interpersonal situations. It's an accessible read that's an invaluable resource for anyone looking to better handle workplace dynamics."

Diane J. Goodman, Ed. D.

Diversity Trainer and Consultant, author of *Promoting Diversity and Social Justice, 2nd Edition*

"Dr. Kathy Obear has developed a method that will save hundreds of jobs, prevent hours of restless nights, and will contribute to building happier, more productive workplaces. And she's presented and written it in such a way that we will be able to begin making changes in our lives the very minute we decide to! Her ability to break down the steps of a reactive triggering event cycle so that we can understand how to proactively slow down or stop harmful thoughts and interactions is transformational. *Turn the Tide* helps us to know that we are not alone in experiencing difficult situations, but we can be the one who respond wisely to them. She has sincerely offered each of us a gift… it is up to us to open it and use it!"

Tanya Williams, Ed. D.
Associate Vice President for Institutional Diversity and Community Engagement, Union Theological Seminary in the City of New York

"This book challenges and guides the reader to pursue self-understanding as a vehicle for hope when faced with conflict and difficult conversations. Beginning to end, *Turn the Tide* is a constant gift modeling compassion, truthfulness, generosity, acceptance and courage. A must read for anyone concerned with authenticity and healing."

Larry D. Roper, Ph. D.
Professor, School of Language, Culture and Society, Coordinator, College Student Services Administration, Social Justice Minor, Oregon State University

"There is much to like and praise in this book. The author's voice in sharing her personal stories makes you feel as if you are in a coaching session with someone who really understands your experience! For those in supervisory positions, modeling the tools in this book about responding effectively in difficult situations will enhance your leadership credibility in a manner that far outweighs any institute or workshop you could experience."

Gwen Dungy, Ph. D.
Executive Director Emeritus, NASPA

"In *Turn the Tide: Rise above toxic, difficult situations in the workplace*, Obear combines everyday real stories with a broad scope of analysis and critical tools that offer ways of making sense of difficult and triggering work situations. Unlike most books in this genre that straightjacket the reader with a one size fits all approach, *Turn the Tide* ignites interest and enables the reader to contextualize content and tools in their own personal and professional lives. Obear writes in an uncomplicated and accessible style and I have no doubt that those who read *Turn the Tide* will realize how long and how much it's been needed. Best of all, the book is grounded in a pro-social justice perspective."

Dennis Francis, Ph. D.
Former Dean of Education, University of the Free State, South Africa

"No one is immune from dealing with negative people or challenging situations. This book offers what few others provide: remedies and techniques to deal more effectively while maintaining your respect for self and others. If you are tired of dealing with stress, professionally or personally, then reading this book is the decision you can make."

Maura. J. Cullen, Ed. D.
Author of *35 Dumb Things Well-Intended People Say,* Diversity & Inclusion Specialist

"*Turn the Tide* is a must read given our current racialized climate. While there are many things that may invoke triggering moments, race is particularly salient at this time. Kathy has done an amazing job outlining the way to move through triggers so we can engage in a way that honors our humanity."

Jamie Washington, M.Div., Ph. D.
President, Washington Consulting Group, Co-Founder, The Social Justice Training Institute

"Many educators, specifically Black Teachers, struggle to navigate difficult situations in schools. Obear's work openly and honestly moves us to examine the underlying issues of power and difference that impact what it takes to navigate those conditions and ultimately make workplaces and schools more inclusive. She provides practical tools that not only focus on action, but also on how we can use our identities and experiences to transform our environments. This is a must read for people working for social change in and outside of schools."

Micia Mosely, Ph. D.

Executive Director, The Black Teacher Project, Faculty Fellow, Institute for Urban Minority Education, Teachers College, Columbia University

"Cultural competency requires us to learn how to respond rather than react, as a way to stay engaged in the conversation and facilitate potential transformation. Dr. Obear teaches us how to do just this as a way to strengthen and sustain relationships. Her stories and examples make this work most accessible and the tools and exercises make this book a must read for anyone invested in creating a more humane and just world."

Patty Perillo, Ph. D.

Vice President for Student Affairs and Assistant Professor of Higher Education, Virginia Tech

"*Turn the Tide* has effective practical examples and application exercises that work. Very empowering! Kathy, you help make the journey possible. Thank you for challenging us to learn about "triggers" and transformation. It is up to each of us to engage in the journey and accept the challenge of reframing our story."

Dawn R. Person, Ed. D.

Professor, Educational Leadership, Director, Center for Research for Educational Access and Leadership (C-REAL), California State University, Fullerton (CSUF)

TURN THE
TIDE

RISE ABOVE TOXIC, DIFFICULT
SITUATIONS IN THE WORKPLACE

BY KATHY OBEAR, ED.D.

DEDICATION

To my fellow travelers on this journey to reclaim our voice and create the life we envision,

I hope you remember you are not alone and there is a way through.

TABLE OF CONTENTS

Introduction

IF YOU ARE LIKE KERRY, THERE IS HOPE.

Kerry arrived at work irritated and thinking about how she had to go tell her supervisor that she still hadn't completed the final report. She was so pissed at her colleague John for dropping the ball and not getting her that last section she needed. She didn't mean to yell at him yesterday, but when he just shrugged when she asked for the report (for the 4th time!), she just snapped and let him have it! She was so tired of being let down by him and everyone else! As she walked by a window she saw her frown in the reflection and knew she should smile more and greet her coworkers as she rushed to her office, but they never seem happy to see her, so why should she bother?

As she took off her coat she saw a message from her boss, Karen, to come see her immediately, and she felt irritated all over again as well as stressed out about what she imagined Karen would say. As she walked to her boss' office she was practicing how she would explain the delay when she bumped into a colleague who spilled his coffee on her blouse. She looked really frustrated as she walked away thinking, "What an idiot! He should watch where he is going!"

Just as she predicted her boss was unreasonable and blamed her for John's incompetence. When Karen said she hoped she wouldn't come to regret giving her this assignment, Kerry stuffed her emotions, smiled, and said she would make it her top priority. She left thinking, "What a ...!! It's not my fault he is so unprofessional and incompetent!"

Back at her desk, she was trying to put together a slide presentation for Friday but couldn't concentrate as she kept replaying her conversation with her boss over and over. She kept rehearsing what she should have said instead of just quietly nodding and smiling through gritted teeth.

As the phone rang, she noticed she was now late to the project team meeting and ran out the door as she answered her cell, stubbing her toe on the doorframe on her way out. When she walked in late the team leader looked irritated. She thought to herself, "He never appreciates all I do for this team or thanks me for busting my tail on this presentation!" When he asked her for an update, she blurted, "I am doing the best I can. I am so overloaded from doing everyone else's job right now, I will get it to you in plenty of time." As she noticed the team's reaction, she felt so embarrassed that she went off like that, and worried that her boss would hear about it. As she rushed out to her 10:30am meeting, Kerry was already feeling exhausted and when she arrived, she realized she had gone to the wrong meeting room.

During the next meeting, Kerry tried twice to make her point and each time a male colleague interrupted her and challenged her ideas. She just shut down, fuming and felt completely disrespected. A few minutes later she heard another man put forth a very similar idea to hers and all of the team seemed to love it! She felt so angry she almost started to cry but swallowed her feelings and put on her game face knowing what people would think of her if she didn't.

Nursing the start of another migraine, she thought, "I used to feel excited to come to work. Maybe it's time to start looking for a new job." Back at her desk, she tried to finish the presentation slides, but she had so little energy, she couldn't concentrate. When John stuck his head into her office with a big smile and asked if she'd reviewed the final section of the report that he sent her, she just stared at him blankly, full of rage, and thought, "When did he expect me to get to that? He was five days late and now he expects me to drop everything just because he finally did his job?!?!" Or did she actually say some of that? Given John's face and his quick exit, she wasn't sure. Later that afternoon, as she was reviewing John's section, she realized she would have to rewrite over half of it and stay late editing so she could get the final report to her boss before she left and avoid disappointing Karen once again.

On her way home she called a friend to commiserate, "Why do I have to work with such unprofessional and incompetent people!? They make me so mad all the time! I don't mean to blow up and be so short with them, but they make me so angry!" As she stopped to get a bottle of wine, she remembered she still had to finish those presentation slides before the next morning and resigned herself to the fact that it would be another long night.

Kerry had no idea why she was so angry all the time or why she seemed to overreact and blast her colleagues. She was increasingly frustrated at how scattered and distracted she was at work. She felt more and more isolated and alone as well as increasingly unappreciated. It seemed her emotions had a life of their own and she couldn't control them anymore. Each day she woke up replaying the scenes from the day before over and over, feeling even more angry, disrespected and taken advantage of.

YOU ARE NOT ALONE

If you are like me or the many people I have coached and trained over the years you probably relate to Kerry in some ways. So many people experience significant conflict at work and have very challenging, toxic relationships with colleagues and supervisors. It is extremely common to feel deep frustration as well as anxiety and self-doubt during difficult work situations. So many people, especially women, not only get angry in difficult conversations but, at the same time, start to question their own competency and wonder if maybe they are at fault. They play the "if only game:" If only I had said it more gently or softly, if only I had smiled more or been less direct, then everything would have been fine. Maybe I am not as competent as I think I am...

While some people can keep their emotions under control most of the time, stuffing our feelings takes a toll on our health and can undermine our ability to think clearly and communicate effectively. While we may be able to keep it together in important meetings or with our manager, we often then overreact and "take it out" on our colleagues and those with less power and status in the workplace or explode at home with our family and friends. Our reactions can undermine working relationships, stifle creativity and team effectiveness, damage our reputation, and possibly impact our future career opportunities.

It can feel overwhelming at times, like there is no solution except to put up with it all and just keep doing our job. Yet there is another way, a way to greater satisfaction, peace, and productivity at work. If you have ever wondered, "Why can't I control my feelings?" or thought, "I never know what will set me off next!" then this book may be useful to you. If you feel stuck, depleted, and tired of all the negative reactions you experience at work, then the tools and strategies in these chapters may help you get the respect and recognition you deserve.

WHY THIS BOOK MAY BE HELPFUL

I can understand why some people may not want to read this book. It can feel scary to take a closer look at why these situations occur. It is far easier to just keep blaming everyone else and hope they might change than to take the risk to look at how we react and explore what responsibility we might have for co-creating these difficult situations.

When our buttons are pushed over and over in difficult workplace situations we may feel burnt out, become more cynical, and think about switching jobs in hopes that the "grass is greener" somewhere else. We may seem less invested in our work and the quality of our productivity and innovation may diminish over time. We might get overlooked for important assignments or promotions if we show up stressed out and frustrated more often than not. Prolonged stress can seriously impact our physical and mental health.

You *can learn* to navigate difficult workplace dynamics with greater ease, clarity, and self-confidence and develop the capacity to speak your truth in ways that helps teams make better decisions and create higher quality products and services. I wish I had learned these skills several decades ago! I may have saved myself countless wasted hours obsessing, as well as thousands of dollars in therapy and self-help books. And, possibly, my career may have moved along more quickly and successfully and I would have been of even greater service to others.

WHO WILL BENEFIT?

I believe this book can be useful to most employees as well as anyone with supervisory or leadership responsibilities. Managers can more effectively supervise others when they both understand why people may over-react or shut down, and then use these skills to coach employees to effectively navigate difficult situations. Managers who model and implement these tools can expect significant improvement in teamwork, innovation, productivity, and customer service. Additionally, they will see far less workplace tension and fewer complaints, conflicts, and time-consuming mediation sessions.

HOW TO GET THE MOST OUT OF THIS BOOK

The concepts and tools in this book reflect the processes I have used for twenty-five years with coaching clients and workshop participants to effectively navigate difficult, triggering work situations. There are a number of ways to use this book. If you need some tools and solutions right now, then you may want to read Chapter 7 about effective ways to respond in the moment, as well as review the Appendix or visit my website for additional resources, www.drkathyobear.com/book-worksheets. Or you may want to read through the book to get an overview of the key concepts and ideas, and then go back and complete the exercises.

To get the most out of this book, I recommend you start at the beginning and read each chapter in order and commit to doing each exercise before you move onto the next chapter. Reading for understanding and knowledge may be helpful to you, but I have found that only actively engaging in all of the activities has resulted in long-lasting change. It is like the difference of reading a book about working out or actually going to the gym for regular exercise. Completing these exercises and applying each of these concepts and tools in your life will be critical if you want to get meaningful results.

Over the years, I have heard so many painful stories of seemingly insurmountable, toxic workplace challenges. And yet, I have also witnessed hundreds of people find relief from the hopelessness and despair by consciously and consistently using these approaches in their daily lives. I hope you give yourself the gift of reading this book with increasing bravery and honesty.

You deserve greater peace and ease in your work life. You deserve to have colleagues, supervisors, and mentors who value and respect you, who are excited to collaborate with you, and who support you to grow to your full potential. Instead of constantly reacting to other people and feeling so frustrated and out of control, you deserve to be in charge of your emotions and actions and create a fulfilling, meaningful work life grounded in purpose, integrity, and joy.

There is hope, there is a way through. I hope you join me on this journey.

Chapter 1

I CAN'T CONTROL HOW I REACT! MAYBE I CAN.

I just snapped. He pushed my buttons. That rubbed me the wrong way. I got hooked! She got under my skin. I reached my boiling point. I was caught off guard. She set me off. I was stopped in my tracks. I blew a fuse. He shut me down. That pushed me over the edge. I was knocked off balance. They rattled my cage. I was ready to explode. Have you ever said or thought any of these phrases?

These are common phrases I hear people use to describe what happens when we lose our composure in the workplace and react unconsciously and impulsively to other people's behaviors. When someone says or does something and we snap it's often because we feel this overwhelming, unexpected rush of intense emotions that comes seemingly out of nowhere. Without thinking, we react on automatic pilot, often in ways that are not very productive as we say and do things we may later regret. Or we stuff our feelings and shut down, and we disappear, but our emotions don't. Most often, they build up over time and come out sideways when we least expect it. In whatever ways we react, our emotions take over and take center stage. They are in charge and we are no longer in control of what we think or how we respond.

When our buttons get pushed, our "reptile brain," the amygdala, takes over and we automatically have fight, flight, or freeze reactions. This part of our brain is trying to protect us from what it interprets as a dangerous situation. Stress hormones are released and we experience immediate physiological changes, including a rush of adrenalin, a racing heart, quicker breathing, and extra blood flowing to the muscles and vital organs. Our senses are sharper and we are revved up on high alert. Now, in a real life-threatening situation, we will be all set to quickly get to safety. Most of the time, we are not in danger, yet the intensity and speed of these stress reactions set us up to react ineffectively in the moment.

In the fight mode, our more aggressive and explosive reactions are counterproductive and may have long-term consequences. Most likely, we create a chain reaction as others react to us in ways that escalate the level of tension, disruption, and team dysfunction. If we freeze, we often feel disoriented and don't know what to say or do. We may be too scared to respond and just shut down and withdraw. We may later judge ourselves for our lack of courage to speak up. If we flee and leave the situation, we may regret the missed opportunity to get involved, interrupt an inappropriate situation, or stand up for what we believe.

Like most people I meet, I never used to recognize what was happening to me when I had these extreme, often disproportionate emotional responses. I believed they were caused by other people and I commonly thought or said things like, "You embarrassed me! You made me so angry! You scared me! You made me cry! You humiliated me!" And since I believed others had caused my feelings, I saw nothing wrong with how I treated them and felt they deserved whatever I did to them in response. Unfortunately, when I reacted unconsciously, I often negatively impacted others in ways that, just like the saying, "What goes around, comes around," brought me negative consequences as well. Here are some of the common "costs" I have heard from clients and workshop participants who reacted on automatic pilot during difficult conversations. See if any of these are familiar.

COMMON FRUSTRATIONS

- Several people are no longer talking to me after that meeting when all I did was give them feedback about the marketing plan.

- I hate all this tension on the team. Why can't people be more professional, stop gossiping, and just speak up like I do?

- I am so exhausted from all this extra work! I hate that management keeps piling it on, but if I say anything, it could hurt my career here.

- It's not my fault I missed that deadline. I had to redo other people's sections. Now my supervisor says he can't depend on me! And when I tried to explain, he got even angrier. I hate this place!

- I am so angry about this new reorganization! Once again, without our input, management made another horrible decision and we suffer the consequences. No wonder some employees want to unionize!

- These competitive jerks are keeping me out of the loop and meeting without me. Just because I told the truth!

- These incompetent people on this team make much more money than I do and do half the work. Yet, I'm expected to clean up their messes with a smile on my face. No wonder I lose it in meetings.

To avoid these consequences, we may wish we had a "do-over", a chance to rewind the tape and try again; or fast forward through our unproductive response and hope no one noticed. Unfortunately, once we have reacted, there is no way to undo our impact.

CORE VALUES

One of the more painful outcomes of my unconscious reactions is that I often treated others in ways that violated my core values. I believe people deserve to be treated with respect, dignity, kindness, and care. When I am more centered and grounded, I usually behave in ways that reflect these values. Unfortunately, in difficult workplace situations I am more likely to react in ways that are counter to these core beliefs. The seductive trap is that reacting in these ways can feel really good in the moment. I have relished the times when I "put him in his place!" or "went off on them." The anger and adrenaline rush feel so good it can be addictive. Yet, afterwards, I have often deeply regretted the long-term impact of these types of unproductive behaviors and the reality that my actions violated the very core values that I espouse and try to model. More disappointing to me is the fact that my inappropriate reactions may have given other people permission to treat me and others in similar demeaning and disrespectful ways.

IT TAKES SIGNIFICANT SKILL TO NAVIGATE DIFFICULT SITUATIONS

In a meeting with colleagues, I was sharing about some new, innovative approaches I was using that I was very excited about. When one person started making fun of me and critiquing what I was doing, my insides exploded. It took everything I had to contain myself and try to get her to stop without fully going off on her. She finally stopped, but then turned away from me. As the group moved on, I was still fuming and had difficulty following much of the next conversation. I was easily provoked several more times in that meeting by most anything she or others said. The atmosphere was tense and stilted, and others seemed to be walking on eggshells. We got little accomplished in that meeting and most people left feeling frustrated.

Toxic workplace situations occur so regularly they have come to be viewed as a normal part of the job. While it is common for us to react unproductively in these moments, it is possible to deal with them in ways without contributing more fuel to the fire. We can actually use tools to de-escalate the tension and dysfunction and lead others towards workable solutions. In these challenging situations we can learn to stay present with our thoughts and feelings and react in ways that are useful, respectful and aligned with our core values. However, in my experience, it takes significant skill to be grounded enough to intentionally choose effective responses. And one of the biggest obstacles is that we rarely realize we are reacting impulsively, much less recognize the impact we are having on others.

Back in 1990, I was co-teaching a course on Facilitating Workshops and was feeling very disappointed with the quality of the participants and their lack of engagement. They came late to the sessions and hadn't done all the homework I had assigned. I felt they didn't respect me or appreciate all the creative tools I was giving them. About half-way through the course, my mentor and co-teacher lovingly gave me some feedback and told me that my content was useful but the way I engaged the participants interfered with their learning. I was shocked by this feedback and worried that I had disappointed him. He said I was coming across as judgmental, self-righteous and controlling and — in his opinion — the participants were shutting down and pulling back in reaction to my behaviors. I had no idea I was coming across in these ways or why my buttons were so easily pushed by the participants. But I definitely wanted them to learn in this course and not let him down, so I was willing to do what was needed.

He helped me begin to reflect on what was going on for me and he wondered if I might be reacting out of fear or old issues from my life. I wasn't so sure, but he offered to pay for me to attend an intensive workshop, "Holding On, Letting Go," that was offered through the National Training Laboratory (NTL). I agreed to attend, possibly out of not wanting to disappoint him any further, and I had a life changing experience. At the workshop I learned how my emotional reactions didn't just happen, but were often fueled by unresolved issues and situations from my past. I began to identify some of the types of comments and behaviors that "pushed my buttons" and learned some tools to interrupt and shift my automatic responses. These were transformative insights for me. I had never realized that I could influence or control my split second reactions in difficult situations, or that other's troubling behaviors might occur, in part, as reactions to my initial unproductive behaviors, like in the Facilitating class I was co-teaching. This was the catalyst for my lifelong passion to teach the tools and skills to react effectively when we have our buttons pushed in difficult conversations.

RATE YOUR TRIGGERS

For the last 25 years, I have used the term "triggered" to describe how we get "hooked" by the comments and actions of others. I used to think that you either felt triggered or you didn't, like going from a dead stop to driving 100 miles per hour. I now realize that the strength of my emotions can range along a continuum and I find it helpful to gauge their intensity using a scale from -10 to +10[1].

A rating of 0 means we have no emotional reaction. This doesn't mean we are numbed out or unaware of our emotions. It means that we did not have any triggered feelings in a situation. Between -3 and +3 we have mild emotions and feel slightly uncomfortable, nervous or irritated. At these lower levels of emotional response we may not like the circumstances we are in, but we generally still have the capacity to notice our feelings and interrupt any urge to react automatically. We can pause to think more clearly and then choose a way to respond that aligns with our core values and the needs of the moment.

We feel "triggered" when our emotions are so unexpected and intense that we are distracted and quickly over-react without conscious thought. A rating of -10 means that we experienced an extreme degree of negative emotions, such as anger, fear, disappointment, grief, embarrassment, defensiveness, or hatred. At +10 we feel extreme positive emotions including excitement, joy, happiness, attraction, enthusiasm, and passion. Even a more moderate level of emotions, between 4–6, can still impact our ability to respond effectively.

When our feelings are extremely high, we probably shouldn't trust our initial perceptions or thoughts. If we have an intense, disproportionate reaction, it is more likely that our response is fueled by cumulative impact or retriggered issues from our past. Any impulsive reaction will usually escalate the difficulty of the situation. In Chapter 5, I highlight some stress management tools you can use to decrease your emotions to a more mild-moderate level from which you can more accurately assess situations and choose effective responses.

I had such a powerful sense of relief and freedom when I finally realized that I did not have to automatically, impulsively react in difficult situations; that I could influence and navigate how I responded when I felt triggered. Through my research, I have identified a predictable series of seven steps that occurs every time we react unconsciously when we feel triggered, "The Triggering Event Cycle©." Instead of feeling out of control and powerless to influence our reactions, we can use The Triggering Event Cycle as a framework to first recognize where we are in the process and then choose the right tools to help us respond effectively in the moment.

The Triggering Event Cycle

1. A stimulus occurs.
2. The stimulus triggers our intrapersonal roots.
3. Our intrapersonal roots form a lens through which we make meaning of what we are experiencing.
4. Our cognitive, emotional, and physiological reactions are shaped by our interpretation of what we experience.
5. The intentions that fuel our reaction are influenced by how we make meaning of the situation.
6. We react to the stimulus.
7. Our reaction may be an additional trigger for others and/or for us.

See if you can relate to the following example and notice how each of the 7-Steps of The Triggering Event Cycle played out in this difficult situation. Maria had just been asked by her supervisor to chair a new project team. During the first meeting, as she was reviewing the overall purpose of the team, one of the older members of the team interrupted her and said, "I'm curious, how did you get picked to lead this group?" (Step 1). She was thrown off balance by the question and felt an immediate wave of anxiety and frustration (Step 4). Her chest and throat felt tight and she thought, "Why is this person trying to embarrass me? Maybe it's because I didn't enthusiastically support his idea in last week's staff meeting." She nervously laughed and said, "Just my luck, I guess!" and redirected the group's attention to the next order of business (Step 6) hoping no one had noticed her initial facial expressions. Later, she realized that she had felt shaky for the rest of the meeting and had trouble concentrating on what people were saying, though she didn't know why (Step 7). As she reflected during our coaching session, she recognized that she had already been feeling nervous about that initial meeting and the team member's comment triggered her own questions about whether she was competent enough or experienced enough to lead this project (Step 2). In addition, she realized how the person reminded her of someone from her college debate team who constantly competed with her and often questioned why she got chosen to take leadership roles (Step 2). She saw that at Step 3 she had created the "story" that this team member was trying to undermine her leadership among the group members. Her intention (Step 5) for reacting by saying, "just my luck," was to avoid any conflict and just push through the agenda. Unfortunately, her unwillingness to directly engage her colleague's question may have left others wondering about her leadership abilities as well (Step 7).

Maria felt disappointed with her reaction and wished she had responded differently. When she kept replaying the situation over in her mind during the meeting (Step 4), she was distracted from the conversation. In our session, she realized that she could have interpreted the situation very differently at Step 3. If she had, instead, assumed that her colleague was being curious, possibly wanting to know what he needed to do to be selected for similar roles in the future, then she may have felt willing to mention the 2 previous projects she had co-facilitated and how her research was related to the focus on this team's goals.

As I describe these Steps in more detail, see if you can recognize where each played out in the previous story. We experience some circumstances at Step 1 that retrigger old issues, fears, or memories at Step 2. I call these "intrapersonal roots." Like the luggage we take on a trip, we bring emotional baggage into workplace situations and these "roots" affect whether or not we feel triggered as well as the intensity of our emotional response. These intrapersonal roots form a "lens" through which we experience the situation or stimulus and influence which aspects of the situation we notice and pay attention to and which facets we don't even see.

At Step 3, we interpret what we see through the lens of the intrapersonal roots and make up a "story" about what we think occurred and why. Often the story we create is far more related to our re-stimulated intrapersonal roots than the actual facts and details of the situation. Our interpretation shapes our initial physiological reactions, feelings, and thoughts at Step 4. At this point, we might begin to recognize we feel triggered, though possibly not. We are often unaware of what occurs at Step 5 when we "choose" the intentions or motives that influence how we react at Step 6. At this point, we still may not be aware how deeply triggered we feel or how unproductively we just reacted. If we have mismanaged the situation, then at Step 7, our actions may be a trigger for others and/or ourselves, and The Triggering Event Cycle repeats as workplace dynamics spiral into greater dysfunction.

Using The Triggering Event Cycle to reflect back on difficult workplace situations helps us to recognize what was influencing our unproductive reactions and identify ways we could have responded more effectively. We can also use The Triggering Event Cycle as we anticipate how we may feel triggered in future situations. We can imagine how we might typically react unproductively and then visualize and practice more useful responses. In the next chapters, I offer more details about each of the 7 Steps to deepen your capacity to use The Triggering Event Cycle as a diagnostic tool during and after difficult situations.

SUMMARY

Even after 25 years of researching and studying difficult situations and triggering events, I still feel unexpected deep emotions and get knocked off my game. The good news is that most of the time I remember to use some of the tools in this book to de-escalate my feelings to a more moderate level so that I can choose productive solutions in the moment. Occasionally, I still unconsciously overreact in ways that undermine my core values, positive intentions, and effectiveness. Luckily, today I have the skills to repair the negative impact of my actions and rebuild relationships to work collaboratively with others to resolve the original problems or issues.

There is a way out and a way through. We do not have to be prisoners of our automatic, triggered reactions. We do not need to feel so irritated, disappointed and anxious with colleagues all the time. We can take charge of our reactions and respond effectively in difficult situations in ways that result in greater productivity, teamwork, innovation, and customer service. The first step is to deepen our awareness of the types of comments and difficult situations that push our buttons.

Chapter 2

STEP 1 — WHAT PUSHES YOUR BUTTONS?

Earlier in my career, I was surprised to realize that not everyone had the same emotional reactions that I did in the same situations. For example, during a presentation that I thought was rather interesting a colleague leaned over and said they were bored to tears. This was curious to me, so I looked around to see what others might be feeling. A few people seemed to be taking copious notes and hanging on the presenter's every word. Another person was trying to hide the fact that they were playing a computer game on their laptop and a couple of others were falling asleep. Then several people abruptly laughed as the presenter was telling a supposedly funny story, but I was so offended I wanted to walk out. Each of us had very different reactions to the same circumstances or "stimulus". So I concluded that everyone must have their own unique types of situations that push their buttons or trigger them. If triggers are "in the eye of the beholder," then it is important that we each identify which types of comments and behaviors are common hot buttons for us, as well as for those with whom we work.

IDENTIFY YOUR COMMON HOT BUTTONS, STEP 1

Below is a sample list of some of the difficult workplace situations that people have shared with me over the years. *For a more extensive worksheet, go to the Appendix or visit my website, www.drkathyobear.com/book-worksheets.* As you read each one, consider how much of an emotional reaction you would most likely have in that situation. Use the -10 to +10 scale I discussed in the previous chapter to rate each item:

Make a personalized list of your highest rated items in a journal or on a separate sheet of paper.

A. When someone (colleague, direct report, supervisor, client, etc.):

- Doesn't do what you ask or doesn't follow your instructions

- Doesn't acknowledge or respect your leadership

- Doesn't follow through on what they said they would do

- Keeps making the same mistakes

- Is not very competent in their job

- Takes credit for your work

- Goes behind your back to undermine you

- Interrupts you or others

- Ignores your ideas

- Loves your idea only after someone else suggests it

- Is belittling or demeaning

- Demonstrates bullying or threatening behavior

- Debates and disagrees with everything you say

- Is more concerned with protecting their "turf" than achieving the overall goals

B. When your supervisor or manager:

- Micromanages and second-guesses you

- Is controlling rather than inspiring and empowering

- Expects that you stop what you are doing and focus on what they want you to do

- Doesn't ask for your input in decisions that affect your work

- Doesn't give you as much guidance and direction as you ask for, and then is highly critical of the outcome you produced

- Avoids making the hard decisions and makes you play the "bad cop"

- Doesn't hold people accountable for low quality work, poor performance

- Expects you to work late and come in early for no additional compensation

- Is only concerned with "moving up the ladder" and "looking good" to the leader

C. When you:

- Make a mistake or an error

- Do or say something inappropriate or offensive

- Don't know what to say or do next

- Believe the conversation is about to "get out of control"

- Have a strong opinion and no one else agrees with you

Not all difficult situations are "negative." We can also feel intense, distracting emotions during seemingly "positive" situations. For instance, if someone is assigned to lead a new major project or gets promoted, they may feel overly excited as well as anxious and nervous that they are not competent enough and they might fail. Or they may be concerned that others will be jealous they were chosen for this exciting "stretch opportunity." In addition, they may be so over-focused on the new opportunity that they are distracted from completing their current job responsibilities.

If you have additional examples of difficult workplace situations to add to this, I would love to hear from you! https://drkathyobear.com/contact

I believe it is critical that we continuously identify our hot button behaviors and comments for two key reasons. We will be able to better anticipate potential difficult situations and, therefore, be more prepared to respond effectively. In addition, we will have greater capacity in the moment to recognize situations when we commonly feel triggered and use the tools in this book to avoid reacting in unproductive ways.

JOURNAL ABOUT DIFFICULT SITUATIONS

I recommend that you start writing about the moments and situations where you feel triggered at work. Use the following prompts to make notes:

- What happened?

- What were you feeling and thinking?

- On the -10 to +10 Scale, how intense were your emotions?

- How did you react? (fight, flight, freeze)

- What was the impact of your reaction on others? On yourself? On the group's goals?

When you reflect back on these journal entries, you can begin to see patterns and common themes. Given your stressful and packed lives, it is too easy to forget the details of these situations or to minimize their importance or impact. These entries will give you a rich source of information and direction for further learning, healing, and growth. My clients who make the most progress keep an active journal and analyze these difficult situations using the tools in this book and, as a result, gain meaningful insights into changes they can make to see immediate results in their work lives.

CUMULATIVE IMPACT

A client I'll call Vanessa woke up in a good mood and felt excited about her new project. Driving to work she was humming along to the radio as she thought about some innovative ideas she could implement. During her first meeting of the day, a colleague interrupted her and she graciously paused for them to make their point, and then continued with what she was saying while she wove their comment in and completed her thoughts. She felt little to no emotional reaction and moved on. Nothing could ruin her good mood, or so she thought. During her next two meetings, she noticed she was feeling mildly irritated as a couple of her female colleagues were each interrupted. In those situations, she redirected the conversation back to them, but the flow and productivity of the meeting were definitely disrupted. By the last meeting of the day, when a male colleague interrupted her, she felt a familiar wave of intense frustration and stopped him with a curt, "I haven't finished my point." As she continued, she realized she didn't feel as clear or focused. And it was clear from her tone that she did not appreciate his behavior.

She had different levels of reactions throughout the day because she was impacted by the cumulative impact of the multiple difficult moments she'd experienced over such a short period of time. The residue and build-up of each situation resulted in her reactivity later in the day.

On reflection, she noticed that the group memberships of her colleagues also contributed to her reaction. The initial interruption came from a female colleague whom she respected and valued. During the rest of the meetings, the interrupters were all male. And in that last meeting, the person who interrupted her fit the profile of the people who she felt had worked to undermine her career: white male leaders in their mid-40s to mid-60s. She noted she is usually less reactive if younger white men interrupt her or if women from any racial group or men of color talk over her.

The social identity group of the person whose behavior is the source of the trigger is usually a significant factor in how emotional we feel. We may be more or less reactive given their combination of group memberships, including their age, hierarchical position, years of experience, race, sex, gender identity, sexual orientation, socio-economic class, disability status, religion/spiritual practice, etc. Given the same behavior, we give some people a pass and the benefit of the doubt while, for others, we have a more intense response.

Exercise

RECOGNIZE CUMULATIVE IMPACT

In your journal, write about a difficult situation where you had a more intense emotional reaction. Then, think back to earlier that day or that week, and identify if you had previously experienced a series of similar situations that may have contributed to your reacting out of the cumulative impact from these multiple experiences.

Exercise

RECOGNIZE THE IMPACT OF SOCIAL
IDENTITY GROUP MEMBERSHIPS

In your journal, use the -10 to +10 scale to note how triggered you might feel given the different social identity groups of the various people involved. In addition, note 1–2 reasons for your varying reactions.

1. Someone challenges and criticizes you as you are making a presentation. Would you feel any differently if the comments came from someone who was a male colleague? Or one of the youngest members of the group? Or a close female friend of yours?

2. Someone is having a side conversation during a meeting while you are talking. Would you feel any differently if the behaviors were from your supervisor? Or from someone who is a different gender or race than you? Or an older, more experienced colleague you do not particularly like?

3. During a casual lunch, a colleague is making demeaning and belittling comments about another co-worker. Would you feel any differently if the colleague is female, male or transgender? A brand new employee? Or the executive secretary to the leader?

Exercise

IDENTIFY THE SOCIAL IDENTITY GROUPS
THAT INFLUENCE THE DEPTH OF YOUR
EMOTIONAL REACTIONS

Think about a difficult workplace situation where you had an intense emotional reaction and make some notes in your journal:

a. Briefly describe the situation

b. How intense was your emotional reaction on the scale
-10 to +10?

c. What were the key social identity groups of the people
involved?

d. Imagine what different social identity groups of those
involved might have resulted in you:

- Feeling less emotional?

- Feeling more emotional?

e. Why do you think you might have these varying reactions, given the different social identity groups of
those involved?

As you continue to reflect on your common triggers, it is
useful to think about the following questions:

- Do I have the same level of emotional reactions to
everyone who exhibits this behavior?

- Are there patterns related to the social identity groups
of the people in these difficult situations when I may
feel more or less emotional?

Identifying these patterns may give you clues to some
of the intrapersonal roots that are fueling your reactions
and may help you better anticipate and prepare for future
workplace situations.

Have you ever entered a roundabout or traffic circle when you were driving and you couldn't figure out how to get off? Just like on a rotary, we can get stuck going around and around in The Triggering Event Cycle and feel like there is no way out. But there are "off-ramps" at each of the Steps, tools we can use to break the cycle and not react unproductively. I want to thank my colleague Sam Killerman for this great metaphor. In the following chapters, I outline Steps 2–7 of The Triggering Event Cycle and recommend specific tools and "off-ramps" that you can use at each Step to respond more thoughtfully and deliberately in difficult situations.

Chapter 3

STEP 2 — INTRAPERSONAL ROOTS

"Life is a train of moods like a string of beads; and as we pass through them they prove to be many colored lenses which paint the world in their own hue, and each shows only what lies in its own focus."

~ RALPH WALDO EMERSON

See if you can relate to the following story a client told me:

I was in a pretty good mood as I was driving to my next meeting when, out of the blue, someone cut me off and nearly hit my car. I felt intense anger and terror and had an immediate flash of memory from 10 years before when I was rear-ended by a drunk driver. I started shaking and sweating and had trouble breathing. I pulled over to the side of the road as soon as I could so that I could calm myself down enough to drive. When I got to the meeting I was still a little shaky...

Most people aren't aware of how their past can get retriggered by current circumstances. I know I wasn't. I thought there were just two steps: You triggered me and I reacted! The truth is that other people's comments and behaviors push our buttons, but we have carried those buttons around, often for a long time. Before I started my research, I had no clue that difficult situations can "re-activate" some of my internal issues and unfinished business, what I call our "intrapersonal roots." I had no understanding of how these roots influence every subsequent Step in The Triggering Event Cycle.

A client I'll call Margaret had finished her presentation to the top leaders and was responding to a question. She had almost completed her answer when her supervisor chimed in and basically repeated all that she had just said. At that point one of the other leaders started to engage him and they both left her completely out of the conversation. She was furious and felt an immediate surge of energy and heat throughout her body. She felt silenced and erased when her manager took over the discussion without referencing or including her. She stuffed her emotions and tried to listen to their conversation. Eventually, she sat down and couldn't seem to find a way to regain her position in the discussion. As we debriefed this situation, she mentioned how her manager often takes over discussions when the women in the division are leading them. When I asked if other situations from her past came to mind as she thought about what happened, she rather easily remembered some unresolved issues, including times, as a young professional, when her ideas were overlooked while the contributions of male peers were discussed at length. I then asked her to search back further and she had a flash of times her older brothers would "tease" her, steal her toys, and yet never get in trouble. Then I wondered how she had been feeling before the presentation and she talked about being nervous and concerned she wouldn't be taken seriously by these top leaders, and that she was pretty tired from being up much of the night with a sick child and was starting to get a scratchy throat herself.

"Don't let us forget that the causes of human action are immeasurably more complex and varied than our subsequent explanations of them."

~ Dostoyevsky

Margaret's reaction to her supervisor's behavior was shaped by her reactivated intrapersonal roots. These roots formed a lens through which she made meaning of the situation and her interpretation created the intensity of her emotions as well as her physiological responses, thoughts, and reactions. Whenever we feel unexpected, intense emotions during a challenging situation, one or more intrapersonal roots have been re-stimulated. We are usually completely unconscious in this process and end up reacting unproductively. Knowing about the power of intrapersonal roots has helped me be more aware and conscious in the moment. If I stay present to myself, I can recognize how my roots are shaping my triggered reactions and have far greater ability to interrupt The Triggering Event Cycle and choose more effective responses. A critical step is to realize that what I am feeling in the moment may have less to do with what is occurring in front of me and more to do with the issues I brought into the situation.

Few people reflect on these intrapersonal processes unless prompted in a counseling, coaching, or training session. It can be hard to readily see the connections between the current situation and our unresolved conflicts, personal issues, traumas, or suppressed emotions from past or more recent life experiences. It's critical to explore these roots if we want the freedom to respond effectively in difficult situations and not be the prisoner of old habitual, automatic reactions. You no longer have to feel out of control and overwhelmed. You can take back your power and choose how you want to respond in every situation.

7 TYPES OF INTRAPERSONAL ROOTS

Through my research I have identified 7 types of intrapersonal roots, many of which were operating in Margaret's scenario:

1. Current life issues and dynamics

2. Cumulative impact of recent experiences

3. Unresolved unfinished business and old wounds

4. Fear

5. Unmet Needs/What I value

6. Ego-driven desires

7. Biases, assumptions, expectations, shoulds, and judgments

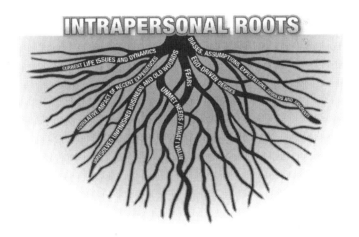

1. CURRENT LIFE ISSUES AND DYNAMICS

When things are going well in our lives, we are less likely to feel triggered by someone's comment or action. Yet, in another moment, when daily stressors build up and deplete our ability to "let things roll off our backs," we may feel deeply triggered. Our protective shield is weakened by the impact of current life issues, including financial concerns, fatigue and burnout, relationship dynamics, illness, problems at work or among family members, deadlines, and angst over national or world crises. When our armor is down or we are preoccupied with competing demands, we are more likely to have stronger emotional reactions in situations where we might otherwise not be as reactive.

Question: A helpful question to ask ourselves in these moments is, "How might the current dynamics and issues in my life be impacting my ability to feel centered and respond effectively in this moment?"

A client told me about a meeting where a colleague was debating and harshly critiquing a point he had just made. Usually, he would listen and ask a few questions to identify openings for possible solutions. Instead, he aggressively matched the energy of his colleague and they launched into a very heated, tense argument that hijacked the purpose and focus of the meeting. As I asked him to reflect on the current life issues that may have depleted his usual protective shield, he talked about how exhausted he felt from all the recent deadlines as well as how distracted he had been with the drama and conflicts of his pending divorce.

Exercise

RECOGNIZING CURRENT LIFE ISSUES

Think about a time you had an intense reaction during a difficult situation and make some notes on the following:

• What are some of the current life issues and dynamics that may have contributed to your susceptibility to feeling triggered?

• How might have these life issues affected the intensity of your triggered reactions?

2. CUMULATIVE IMPACT OF RECENT EXPERIENCES

This intrapersonal root involves the cumulative impact from similar situations that occur within a short period of time, like the "final straw." Imagine that a glass represents the degree of emotions you are feeling. The first time you feel triggered when someone questions your competence, the glass fills halfway with water. The second time it happens that same day, the water rises to just below the top. The third time, you feel someone is questioning your abilities, the water overflows. This is cumulative impact.

If we hold in or stuff our emotional reactions to earlier incidents, our feelings build up over time. The intensity of our triggered reaction in the moment may be disproportionate to the current circumstance because we are reacting out of the cumulative impact of several previous situations. The same people may have been involved in each situation or possibly different people. The incidents may have happened to us or to people we know and care about.

Question: Helpful questions to explore if we are experiencing cumulative impact include, "How does this situation feel familiar? and "When have I felt this way in the recent past?"

Exercise

RECOGNIZING CUMULATIVE IMPACT

Think about a time you felt triggered that may have been related to cumulative impact. Make some notes in your journal:

On a scale of -10 to +10:

- How triggered did you feel the first time it happened?

- The second?

- The third?

- The fourth?

- How effectively did you respond each time?

3. UNRESOLVED UNFINISHED BUSINESS AND OLD WOUNDS

"One faces the future with one's past."

~ Pearl S. Buck

In the past, I would often have an intense reaction in meetings and presentations when others used terms or phrases I did not understand or when they spoke in very abstract ways. I felt like I was being "talked at" and I would feel irritated. I was very critical and judged them as arrogant and out of touch, while at the same time, I felt less than and not as smart. This is a common pattern when we are triggered: we often judge or blame others or critique and shame ourselves, or do both at the same time.

During a period of self-healing work I made a connection between these common triggers and some unresolved anger and shame related to my father. I have painful memories of sitting through lectures from him at the dinner table about issues and theories I didn't understand. Instead of creating a participative environment where I could engage and learn with him, he used one-way communication that left me feeling inferior, small, and voiceless. As I have resolved these old issues as well as others related to him, I am far less likely to feel triggered in the same way during one-way lectures and presentations. Today, I may not prefer this type of experience nor easily learn this way, but I rarely retrigger those old feelings of inferiority or shame.

"I may have pushed my buttons, but I didn't install them."

~ Marshall Rosenberg

A client I'll call Sherry shared an example of re-stimulated old wounds that occurred when she was preparing to facilitate a training session. While participants were getting settled before the start of the program, she was writing on a chart pad and heard a voice that seemed familiar. She immediately felt terror and flashed back to when she was sexually abused in her youth. When she looked at the man whose voice had retriggered her old trauma she realized that he was far too young to have been the abuser those decades before, and yet she could not shake her feelings of fear and danger for the rest of the session.

Current situations can reactivate memories and emotions from our past. If we do not feel resolved around past situations, it is like we wear them on our bodies like buttons that can be pushed by others. When situations "hook our history," we have difficulty staying present and may unconsciously relive the past event in the moment. As a result, our triggered reactions are more directly connected to these unresolved issues, and not necessarily to what is occurring in the present moment.

There are a wide variety of possible types of unresolved issues, including those we personally experienced or those we observed happening to others. Some sources include dysfunctional family dynamics (neglect, abandonment, abuse, sibling rivalry, unrealistic expectations, parental domination); violations of our boundaries through bullying and violence (physical, emotional, sexual, and spiritual); acts of humiliation or betrayal we experienced; times we were denied fair access or opportunities; experiences of discrimination and oppression; the death of people or animals we valued; and the abuse of power or position by authority figures in our lives.

We are usually unaware of how we have merged unresolved issues, emotions, and perceptions from our past with the current triggering event. These connections can become more clear with honest reflection and the willingness to take responsibility for our reactions. *Go to the Appendix for a worksheet to help you explore and identify unresolved issues and old wounds.*

"Whenever you are about to find fault with someone, ask yourself the following question: What fault of mine most nearly resembles the one I am about to criticize?"

~ Marcus Aurelius, *Meditations*

A related facet of this root involves aspects of our own behavior that we are uncomfortable with. I remember feeling so angry when a leader was micromanaging me. While talking to a friend, she reminded me how I recently had received feedback that I supervised others in a very similar way. After that feedback, I realized I didn't like how I was over-managing and being hypercritical of others. Seeing what I did not like about myself reflected back in the behavior of others gave me the opportunity to experience how others may have felt when I was micromanaging them. At the time, I didn't appreciate this lesson, but later I used it as an impetus to change my style and approach to management.

Exercise

WHEN OTHERS MIRROR OUR BEHAVIORS

In your journal, list 4–5 characteristics or behaviors that you do not like in others.

-

-

-

-

-

Then think about a time you felt triggered when someone displayed one or more of these behaviors or characteristics.

- How did you react?

- When have you displayed similar behaviors or characteristics? How are you similar to this person?

- In the past, when your reactions resembled those of the person involved in this challenging situation, what could you have done that would have been more productive?

If we are aware and willing, we can use these times when the behaviors of others mirror our own as opportunities to refocus on ourselves and shift our actions so they better align with our core values and positive intentions.

Question: During the times you wonder if a current situation may have re-stimulated old issues and wounds, it is useful to ask yourself, "How, if at all, does this situation remind me of any old, unresolved issues or past traumas?" and "Who comes to mind as I think about the possible connection between the current situation and old issues or wounds?" and "How is this person a mirror of me?"

I believe it takes courage and inner strength to reflect on the possible old issues and wounds that fuel our triggered reactions. In my experience, I often stir and re-awaken memories that I have long buried. I am so grateful for the therapists, coaches, and friends who have supported me on my journey to greater healing and wholeness. I hope you find powerful supporters to help guide you on your path.

4. FEARS

"Courage is not the absence of fear, but rather the judgment that something else is more important than fear."

~ Ambrose Redmoon

When we carry any fear or anxiety into a difficult situation we are more likely to feel triggered than during times we are more centered, grounded, and confident. A colleague of mine was deeply concerned as he sat down at the head of the table. He hadn't known the senior vice president would be attending his presentation. He was convinced the SVP would think he wasn't competent enough to lead this critical project. As he began to pitch the team's recommendations about this new initiative, his voice quivered and he stumbled over his words. When the SVP asked a question, he started to sweat when he couldn't find the section in the report that addressed the concerns and he lost his train of thought. He knew he was in trouble when the SVP glanced over at his manager. This example shows when we unconsciously react out of anxiety and fear, we often behave in ways that end up creating the exact circumstances we worried would occur.

CATEGORIES OF FEAR AND ANXIETY

Deepening our capacity to identify the types of fears that drive our triggered reactions can help us more quickly recognize and shift them in the moment and increase our ability to choose courage over fear. Among the seemingly endless types of anxiety and fear, these categories help me recognize this intrapersonal root when I feel triggered:

Competence (What if I lose credibility? I don't know enough; I can't handle this; What if I make a mistake? They will see how incompetent I really am!)

Control (People will get too emotional; This conversation will get out-of-hand; I will be overwhelmed; I have to stay in control!)

Belonging and connection (People will not like me; They will reject me; I will be all alone; I'll let people down and they will be disappointed in me; I will be misunderstood)

Safety and security (People could get hurt; What if I can't protect them? What if they attack me?)

Effectiveness (Things won't change; Things will be worse off than before; I have to do this perfectly! What I do doesn't matter)

Worthiness (What if I am a fraud? Maybe I'm not good enough or talented enough; Maybe I should not be doing this work at all)

Question: It is important that we identify the fears and anxieties that could be the root of our triggered reactions. Helpful questions to ask include, "What am I afraid could happen?" and "What am I afraid of losing?" After recognizing each fear, it can be useful to use the tool, the "Ladder of Fear," to search for any deeper issues or anxieties by asking over and over, "So if this fear were to come true, then what else am I afraid could happen?" *Go to the Appendix for a worksheet to help identify some of your common fears.*

5. UNMET NEEDS/WHAT I VALUE

I am grateful to Marshall Rosenberg for his work in NVC, Nonviolent Communication, where he identified a full range of universal human needs. If some of our core needs or values are not being met in a situation, we could feel triggered. For example, if someone raises their voice in a meeting saying, "That's a stupid idea," then someone may feel upset because this behavior violates their values for respect in the workplace. And the person who had offered the original idea may feel angry and shut down because their needs for recognition and collegiality were not met. Some of the needs and values that seem particularly related to the triggering events I experience include dignity, respect, trust, integrity, safety, belonging, acceptance, honesty, connection, mutuality, partnering, ease, fairness, understanding, recognition, competence, consideration, equity, and inclusion.

The same challenging situation may impact several people differently depending upon which of their unmet needs are re-stimulated in the moment. For example, if a supervisor aggressively talks over a direct report in a meeting, the staff member may feel irritated from having unmet needs related to clarity, respect, and recognition, while a peer observing the situation may feel triggered because their needs for safety, consideration, and mutuality were unmet.

Question: When we feel triggered, it is helpful to pause and search for any of our unmet needs or values. Helpful questions include, "What might be my unmet needs in this moment?" and, "What do I value that is not being honored right now?"

6. EGO-CENTERED DESIRES

"I look in the mirror through the eyes of the child that was me."

~ Judy Collins

Earlier in my career, I was very attached to what people thought of me and I really wanted to be liked. As a result, I would smooth over any hint of conflict or disagreement. If any tension arose, I would make a joke and try to "keep things light" and downplay any difference of opinion in order to gain another's approval and acceptance. As I reflected on this pattern, I realized that this was very similar to how I often reacted to family dynamics in my youth.

As many of us were growing up we may have learned some very useful skills and tools to take care of ourselves and navigate our lives. However, it is also common that we developed some unproductive survival strategies in response to any number of dysfunctional and unsafe situations. While some of these beliefs, assumptions, and behaviors may have helped to keep us out of harm's way in the past, it is likely they are no longer productive approaches in our current life.

I use the term "ego-driven desires" to describe this intrapersonal root and the constellation of dysfunctional thoughts, beliefs, and attitudes that often fuel ineffective triggered reactions. In contrast to the needs and values that add value to our lives and those of others, these ego-driven desires often result in win-lose, power-over situations that only "benefit" some at the expense of others. We may get an ego-hit or an artificial sense of power or belonging in these situations, but our triggered reactions will usually undermine any of our positive intentions and outcomes. When we are motivated by ego-driven desires, our behaviors are fueled by one of these three types of unproductive desires that are inflated, overblown human needs: power and control, status and approval, and belonging and admiration. *Go to the Appendix for a worksheet to identify these in greater detail.*

Question: In moments when our triggered reactions are fueled by ego-driven desires we are over-focused on getting what we want and may have little or no concern for the needs of others or how our behaviors negatively impact them. Questions to examine if we are reacting out of ego-driven desires, include: "Am I focused on what would be helpful to others or on what I think should happen, regardless of the impact on them?" and "Am I more concerned about how I will be judged and evaluated than on achieving the productive goals and outcomes?" and "Am I over-emphasizing my desire for acceptance, approval, and control with little thought to how my actions impact others?"

7. BIASES, ASSUMPTIONS, EXPECTATIONS, SHOULDS, AND JUDGMENTS

Whether we know it or not, we all carry baggage with us into every situation that is full of our biases, assumptions, expectations, shoulds, and judgments. Most of these attitudes and beliefs are grounded in our past experiences and cloud our ability to accurately assess what is occurring in the present moment.

In the early 1990's I was preparing to co-facilitate my first significant workshop at a national conference on diversity in the workplace. The topic was Creating Inclusive Environments for Gay, Lesbian, and Bisexual Employees. A few weeks before the conference there was a vote in the city hosting the event to rescind the current law that prohibited discrimination based on sexual orientation. When I heard that the people of that city had successfully voted to reinstate discriminatory practices in housing and employment, I was far angrier than I recognized. Unconsciously, I assumed that many of the participants who would attend the workshop were homophobic heterosexuals who had voted to overturn the nondiscrimination policy. When I "welcomed" the 300 people to the session, my energy was so angry, judgmental, hostile, and toxic that over half the people left at the break. I doubt anyone learned anything helpful from me that day. My ungrounded assumptions, biases, judgments, and expectations fueled my totally inappropriate reactions and completely undermined my hoped for outcomes.

Questions I wish I had asked myself long before that day include, "What assumptions, biases, and judgments might be affecting my assessment?" "What shoulds and expectations am I placing on others, on myself?" And, "What is my 'pay-off' for holding onto these biases, shoulds, and judgments?"

Go to the Appendix for a worksheet to explore these concepts further.

I believe it takes significant courage to explore your intrapersonal roots and identify why you might feel triggered. It is far easier to blame others and swirl in your triggered emotions. Yet the way out is clear: When we recognize how our retriggered intrapersonal roots fuel how we make meaning of situations and, therefore, how we react unproductively, then, and only then, can we interrupt The Triggering Event Cycle and create a more productive end to the story. Speaking of "story," in the next chapter I explore how we interpret and make meaning of situations at Step 3.

Chapter 4

STEP 3 — MAKING MEANING: CHANGE YOUR STORY, CHANGE YOUR REACTIONS

"We either make ourselves miserable or we make ourselves strong. The amount of work is the same."

~ CARLOS CASTANEDA

I woke up startled and immediately felt deeply anxious as I realized my alarm hadn't gone off and I was an hour late to an important meeting! This was a disaster! As I put on my glasses I realized I had misread the clock and it was actually two hours earlier than I had thought. I felt relieved and delighted. The clock hadn't actually changed. It was my interpretation of what I thought I saw that created my different emotional reactions. Thinking I was late, I felt extremely stressed and irritated. Realizing I was up before the alarm, I was eager to go back to sleep.

At Step 3 of The Triggering Event Cycle, we make meaning of what we are observing through the lens of the intrapersonal roots that have been re-stimulated. As you read the following example, notice which (if any) of the people you most relate to:

Julie was completely caught off guard by the announcement that Shaun was promoted to Vice President. Given what her manager had told her last week, she thought the job would be hers. She was furious! She had more experience, had managed a much larger division, and had led several more major projects teams, and yet, once again, another white male was promoted over her. Maybe it was time to dust off her resume. When Deborah heard about Shaun's promotion she was happy for him as well as for her future possibilities. Since he had informally used her as a co-lead of a recent project, maybe the top leaders would finally know how valuable she could be to the organization. Jeff was very excited about his buddy's promotion and chuckled thinking that Shaun's monthly golf game with the Senior Vice President had paid off! And now with Shaun at the table with the executives, Jeff was feeling very hopeful that he would be the next one to be promoted. Rob just couldn't believe the news. How could they have made Shaun a VP after he mismanaged that team project last year? Everything would have fallen apart if Deborah hadn't taken over. Now Rob was worried about how honest he had been in Shaun's 360 evaluation. If he ever found out about the negative feedback, Shaun might make his life miserable.

Each of these people interpreted the same circumstance, Shaun's promotion, through the lens created by their intrapersonal roots. All of them made up a "story" about what they thought was occurring; and their story fueled their feelings and reactions. We "create our own reality" by how we choose to make meaning and interpret situations we encounter. Our story creates our feelings, the physiological "warning signs" that we are triggered, and our thoughts about ourselves and others. We are usually unaware of why we created this interpretation and we rarely question its validity or explore the intrapersonal roots that fueled our meaning making. We accept our story as "fact" and are often unaware of how it results in triggered emotions and unconscious reactions.

THE POWER OF CHANGING OUR STORY

If we change our initial story, we change our reactions. I remember a time I had a few questions for my supervisor so I sent her an email and copied in the team so they would directly get the same information I did. I was still unclear after she wrote back so I sent a follow-up email with a few more questions. She immediately responded in ALL CAPS! I felt like she was yelling at me. I felt angry and embarrassed that my team saw her reaction. I did not deserve to be treated that way! All I did was ask for greater clarity so I could do my job! The rest of the morning I obsessed about the situation and tried to figure out what I should do. I took a walk during lunch to clear my head. I called a friend for advice and she helped me try to see the situation from my manager's perspective and wondered if maybe she was especially stressed or triggered by something else in her world, or maybe she didn't realize the CAP tab was on when she replied. As I considered my friend's thoughts, I felt less angry and more open to these possible scenarios. As I headed back to the office, I got the idea to stop by my manager's office and check-in with her. As we talked, she mentioned how overwhelmed she was feeling and how grateful she was that I had such a good handle on this project. When I mentioned her email and how she responded in all CAPS, she looked surprised and apologized. She said she was moving so quickly this morning and she would send a quick follow-up email to counter the earlier one. I felt relieved and back on track.

During workshops and coaching sessions I spend a lot of time focusing on shifting our stories and I am often asked, "What if my original story at Step 3 was accurate? Why should I change it?" In these situations I am reminded of that saying, "Do you want to be right or to be happy?" I usually respond with the following points, "You could be right. And, how do you react out of the triggered feelings you created by your 'accurate' story?"

Shifting our interpretation is not about being right or wrong about the other person's intentions. I change how I make meaning of a situation to de-escalate my emotions and create a more grounded space from which to respond. From this more centered place, I am more effective as I engage others, whatever their intentions. When I rewrite my assumptions and interpretations in ways that result in my feeling more curious, compassionate, and empathetic, then I tend to choose more productive responses.

I remember watching the TV show "Dragnet" in my youth and it always seemed one of the detectives was saying to people they were interviewing, "Just the facts, ma'am, just the facts." When I feel triggered, I most often have made up a story based on just a few pieces of data that I have selectively observed. Once I recognize I am triggered, it can be very helpful to put aside my interpretation and assumptions, and refocus on the actual "facts" of the situation I had noticed as well as explore if there are any that I had overlooked.

REVISE YOUR STORY AND TURN THE TIDE

I remember feeling rather impatient in a meeting that was moving more slowly than I had time for that day. As we were figuring out how to fix an unexpected problem, I suggested we pull together a short-term task force to identify a set of recommendations. Right after I spoke someone said, "Another way of proceeding might be..." and I felt even more irritated that he was trying to upstage me. As I noticed I was about to interrupt him and expand on my point, I luckily stopped myself, knowing I was feeling triggered. I "hit pause" for a moment and noticed my depth of frustration and how revved up my energy was in the moment. I realized my initial thought that he was trying to upstage me was clearly an assumption and the fact was that he had merely started to offer another idea. I then remembered that he had turned to me as he spoke with a tone that now seemed more connecting, not undermining. I began to wonder if maybe he was trying to build on my suggestion and, as a result, I felt more open to what he was saying. I was then able to refocus on the conversation as I asked him to say more about how he thought this could help us solve the current problem. Once I shifted my initial story, I was able to remember additional data, de-escalate my emotions, and re-engage in a more productive way. We don't have to react out of our triggered emotions; instead, we can shift our story and create new, more useful feelings that help us expand our vision and explore alternative responses that may be more useful in the moment.

Exercise

PRACTICE SHIFTING YOUR INITIAL STORY

Below are some examples of how to shift the initial story at Step 3 so that you de-escalate your triggered emotions. After you review the first couple of examples, practice rewriting the rest of the interpretations in your journal.

1. If your initial story at Step 3 is, "He is trying to undermine me," then you can de-escalate your emotions by shifting your interpretation to, "Maybe he has a legitimate question; let's see where this goes."

2. If your assumption is, "She stole my idea and is passing it off as her own," you can get more centered by shifting it to, "Maybe she didn't hear me say it just now....I can connect her comment to my earlier one and keep the conversation moving."

3. Practice shifting these stories:

- "He deliberately kept me out of the loop!"

- "She is trying to bully us into agreeing with her plan!"

Exercise

SHIFT YOUR REACTIONS BY CHANGING
YOUR STORY

Shifting your interpretation results in your feeling less triggered and opens up energy and space to choose a productive response. Reflect on the following prompts as you write about a recent difficult situation:

- Describe "just the facts" of the situation, the circumstances.

- What did you make it mean? What "story" did you make up about what you thought was happening?

- How was your story shaped by any intrapersonal roots?

- When you thought this initial story:

    - What were your feelings?

    - What were your physiological reactions?

    - And what thoughts did you have about:

- Yourself?

- Others?

- The situation?

- What unproductive reactions were you considering?

- How does this story serve you? What is the "pay-off"?

- How do you want to feel?

- Shift your story: Create a different interpretation that leaves you feeling less triggered and possibly more open, receptive, and curious.

- Re-imagine the same situation, but with your new interpretation, your new story.

  - How would you feel?

  - What are your physiological reactions?

  - What are your thoughts about yourself, others, and the situation?

  - What potentially more productive responses might you consider from this new perspective?

Go to the Appendix for a worksheet exploring how shifting our story at Step 3 impacts how we react.

If we notice we feel triggered early enough in The Triggering Event Cycle, we can change our initial interpretation, scale back our emotions, and turn the tide before we experience too many dysfunctional thoughts and physiological reactions. However, if we miss this opportunity, the power of our triggered story will propel us to Step 4 where it is much more difficult to interrupt and shift the speed and momentum of our unproductive reactions.

Chapter 5

STEP 4 — COMMON PHYSIOLOGICAL, EMOTIONAL, AND MENTAL REACTIONS

"It is the mind that makes the body."

~ SOJOURNER TRUTH

A client of mine was rather anxious about his upcoming performance review that was scheduled in an hour. While he had a solid track record of success over the years, his most recent project had stalled and one of his direct reports had recently created a huge fiasco for the organization. As he was finalizing his thoughts about his accomplishments and professional goals for the coming year, he noticed that his mind was racing and his heart was beating out of his chest. He was trying to anticipate every possible critique from his leader and was formulating how he could possibly counter each one. One of his team members knocked at his door with a pressing crisis and he moved into triage mode to help find a solution. Afterwards, he realized how good it felt to solve critical problems and how competent he felt as a leader. In the last few minutes he had before his review, he decided to quiet his mind and remind himself of his strengths and capacities. He envisioned his boss giving him some negative feedback and he imagined himself asking for more context and looking for ways he could improve. As he walked in to meet with his supervisor, he felt centered and open. Ironically, 95% of the feedback was positive and he completely agreed with the 1-2 concerns his leader raised. If he had continued to anxiously spiral with all those negative thoughts, he might have entered the session very defensive and guarded and his negative energy might have impacted how his review turned out.

How we make meaning of a situation at Step 3 influences the types of physical reactions, emotions, and thoughts we experience at Step 4. Most people do not recognize they are triggered until they begin to notice their body sensations and emotions, though many still do not know it even then. If we realize we feel triggered at this point, we can use a variety of tools to shift our thoughts, feelings, and physiological reactions in order to make more intentional responses. But we first need to be present enough to notice we are triggered and conduct a "systems check." Just like a doctor will order an x-ray, we can scan ourselves to heighten our awareness of all of our reactions in the moment.

WARNING SIGNS

"The ability to observe without evaluation is the highest form of intelligence."

~ Jiddu Krishnamurti

Our physiological reactions can serve as an early signal that we are deeply triggered. Most people, in retrospect, can identify a number of their personal warning signs, such as when their mind races, their heart pounds, their face flushes, they feel a rush of heat, their fists clench, they have difficulty breathing, or they physically shut down and pull away. When I am triggered I often have a general sense of "grrrr" throughout my upper body and feel a surge of energy and urgency to respond.

For people who struggle to identify these signals, it can be very useful to ask your colleagues and friends for help since, most likely, they have been on the receiving end of your reactions! You can ask, "How do you know I am feeling triggered? What are my nonverbal reactions and warning signs that I am triggered?" Asking for feedback may give you insight into some of your more unconscious signals, including eye twitching, fidgeting, a certain "look," pushing your chair away from the table, pointing your finger at others, clenching your jaw, or rolling your eyes. Increasing your awareness of early warning signs can increase the chance that you recognize you feel triggered before you react in ways you later regret.

Exercise

IDENTIFY YOUR COMMON PHYSIOLOGICAL
REACTIONS

Take a moment to get quiet, comfortable and relaxed.
Close your eyes and remember a difficult work situation
where you felt deeply triggered. Then journal about the
following:

- What body sensations did you notice in your chest?
  Neck? Head? Stomach area? Arms and legs?

- What other physiological responses did you have?

- As you reflect on other difficult situations, what are
  additional body sensations and physical reactions
  you often have?

Our physiological reactions are caused by the rush of
adrenaline we experience when our amygdala, the "reptile brain", is triggered into a fight, flight, or freeze reaction. We can counter these instinctive reactions if we pay
attention to our early warning signals and use stress management tools to interrupt these automatic responses.

TOOLS TO LET OFF STEAM

Like a teakettle that is about to whistle, we can "let off a
little steam" with some quick physical activities, including stretching, rolling our neck and shoulders, and taking a brisk walk. If you are unable to leave a meeting,
there are some techniques you can do under a table or

internally so no one can see, such as clench and release your fists a few times, reposition your body and stance to appear more relaxed and centered, roll your toes in and out over and over, refocus your attention on a piece of art in the room or on some nature or the horizon out the window, and breathe slowly and deeply at least 5 times while concentrating on your breath. If I can take notes easily, I often will write a few thoughts over and over to center myself, like "This will work out eventually" and "I have handled this before."

When using these tools doesn't release enough stress, then I often will find a way to take a break. I can literally ask for a break in the meeting and then find a quiet space to do a more meditative visualization. I can imagine a scene where I always feel calm and centered, such as a quiet beach on a warm, sunny day or I can visualize myself responding in ways that lead to a productive outcome of the situation. When we refocus our mind in ways that leave us feeling more positive or at least more neutral, then we can observe and shift our triggered thoughts and emotions, rather than being driven by them.

IDENTIFY YOUR RANGE OF EMOTIONS

Mike was caught off guard in the leadership team meeting when the vice president announced a major change in practice that would significantly affect his operation. He looked around and noticed no one else looked very surprised. He spoke up and asked the leader to say more about his intended outcomes and how he came to this decision. As he continued, it became all too clear that the leader had made this decision with a few of Mike's peers when they had been traveling together last week. He was incensed at being left out of the decision-making process, yet now expected to implement the new direction. When he started to ask a few more questions to explore the unintended impacts in his area, the leader cut him off and said there were a couple more critical issues to discuss before they ran out of time. Mike felt diminished, overlooked, and discounted in that moment. He thought about pushing back one more time, but given the intensity of his feelings, he decided a better tactic might be to stop by to talk with the leader later that day.

When we feel deeply triggered, we often experience a variety of emotions, though we may not be able to identify them at the time. It is important to increase our capacity to be aware of our feelings in the moment so we can recognize when they seem out of proportion to the current circumstances or possibly fueled by our intrapersonal roots. If we can use some tools to take this off-ramp at Step 4, we may be able to avoid reacting in ways we later regret.

Exercise

IDENTIFY YOUR TRIGGERED EMOTIONS

We usually experience a wide range of intersecting emotions when we feel triggered, including those we may consider to be both "negative" and "positive." Reflect on a recent difficult workplace situation and use the following to make a list of the feelings you experienced. Participants in my workshops are often surprised by how many different emotions they felt in the short span of a single triggering event.

Angry, frustrated, agitated, irritated

Embarrassed, ashamed

Guilty, remorseful

Scared, anxious, nervous, uneasy, concerned

Distrustful, apprehensive

Sad, depressed, disappointed

Judgmental, disgusted

Defensive, guarded

Confused, unsure

Powerless, helpless

Exhausted, overwhelmed

Bored, disinterested

Indignant, hurt

Surprised, caught-off guard

Enthusiastic, excited, inspired

Overjoyed, ecstatic

Attracted, connected

Empathetic, compassionate

Honored, humbled

Grateful, appreciative

Go to the Appendix for a more comprehensive list of emotions.

If I notice I have a mild to moderate range of emotions between -5 and +5, I may still be present enough to make conscious choices. When I experience more intense emotions, I am more likely to be distracted and overwhelmed and react in ways that do not align with my core values.

UNPACK YOUR BAGGAGE

Exercise

EXPLORE WHAT YOU "BROUGHT" TO
THE SITUATION

Another powerful tool when you recognize your emotions at Step 4 is to use the following prompts to tease out how you might be contributing to your reactions.

Reflect on the situation you used in the previous exercise as you consider the following:

- Why was I so triggered then? What else was going on for me (current life issues, cumulative impact, unfinished business)?

- Is what I am feeling directly related to what is happening right now? Or fueled by old issues and past experiences?

- Which of my values and needs were not being met in this interaction?

- Who did this person remind me of?

- I wonder if I did something earlier that triggered them...

If you recognize that the current circumstances retriggered stuffed emotions or old issues, it can be helpful to create safe spaces to explore and express these emotions so you minimize the impact they have on your ability to assess what is actually happening in the moment.

Another category of early warning signals at Step 4 is the thoughts we have about ourselves, others, and the situation. These thoughts are extensions of the initial story we created at Step 3 and are often fueled by our retriggered intrapersonal roots. When I am triggered, I often keep replaying these negative thoughts over and over like a hamster running on a wheel. If we are unable to recognize the barrage of negative thoughts at this Step, we will likely experience a downward spiral of emotions that will undermine our concentration and productivity.

The direct reports of her counterpart kept coming to Rosa with their questions. She initially didn't mind helping them out, but it was now taking time away from her own team and key projects. She mentioned this to her colleague and he said, "Oh yea, thanks. I have been so swamped by this major deadline. In fact, I have to get to another meeting." As he ran out the door she was indignant and thought, "How dare you think you are so much more important than I am! So arrogant and condescending! They are coming to me because you are incompetent and gave them the wrong information to start with! And you keep taking advantage of me because you know I won't turn them away. You should never have been promoted to this management level!"

There are five categories of unproductive thoughts at Step 4. See which of Rosa's thoughts fit into these:

1. **Judgments of others** ("She is so patronizing," "How can he be so rude and immature?" and "They just don't get it!")

2. **Judgments of self** ("I am so incompetent," "How could I make such a horrible mistake?" and "I am letting people down.")

3. **Expectations and "shoulds"** ("I should be perfect," "They should know how to handle this," "She should

maintain control," and, "They should never disrespect me, much less in public!")

4. **Absolute thinking** ("I don't know what I am doing," I can't do anything right," "They are totally incompetent," and "They are a horrible person.")

5. **Victim stances** ("They attacked me!" "He is trying to humiliate me," and "She is out to get me.")

Exercise

IDENTIFY COMMON NEGATIVE THOUGHTS AND SELF-LIMITING BELIEFS

Our negative thoughts at Step 4 are like a song on a CD that is stuck in repeat mode. They will keep replaying over and over until we reject them and replace them with a new CD or a playlist from iTunes! But we first need to recognize the old songs that may need updating. Think about several challenging situations and, in your journal, make a list of some of your common negative thoughts and self-limiting beliefs. Note how you felt when you think these.

Go to the Appendix for a more comprehensive list of negative thoughts and self-limiting beliefs.

The truth is, if someone else said to me all the negative things I think about myself or others, I would never tolerate it. Yet, it almost seems normal to have this endless stream of criticisms and judgments as background music as I go about my day. If we can increase our awareness of these negative thoughts, we can shift them in ways that will de-escalate our emotional and physiological reactions.

"I no longer agree to treat myself with disrespect. Every time a self-critical thought comes to mind, I will forgive the Judge and follow this comment with words of praise, self-acceptance, and love."

~ Miguel Ruiz

As a kid, I loved playing with an Etch A Sketch. I could doodle and draw and then just shake it and quickly erase it all so I could start over. I often wish my mind would work in the same way. I am just glad my negative thoughts don't appear in a bubble over my head where others could see them.

Exercise

SELF-MANAGEMENT TOOLS ~ CHANGE YOUR THOUGHTS

The unproductive, self-limiting thoughts we have during difficult situations decrease our effectiveness in the moment. When we change these thoughts, we are better positioned to choose effective responses. Below are some examples of how to change negative thoughts at Step 4:

1. When I think, "They're not getting it! This is a failure" I can shift my thoughts to, "I will do the best I can. I am not responsible for everyone's learning. People will take away from this what they need."

2. If I think, "I should know the answer to that," then I can change it to, "I am not the expert here. My role is to facilitate the team's creativity. I can tell them I don't know and ask others for their input."

In your journal, practice changing the following negative thoughts:

•   You are such a jerk for interrupting me!

•   I can't handle this!

•   What if I make a fool of myself?

Next, think about a recent triggering situation and write down several unproductive thoughts you had at that time about yourself and others. Then, identify alternative thoughts that could leave you feeling less triggered, if not more open and curious.

Using these self-management techniques at Step 4 will help us stay present to what is actually happening in the moment, instead of obsessing about the negative, self-limiting thoughts in our mind.

Go to the Appendix for more practice shifting negative self-talk and limiting beliefs.

When we consciously choose where we put our attention, our body and our mind follow. By shifting our mental chatter, we can moderate our emotions and our physical reactions.

Exercise

SHIFT YOUR THOUGHTS, SHIFT YOUR FEELINGS

Get in a comfortable position and think about a recent difficult work situation where you had an intense emotional reaction. Focus on the many negative thoughts you had about others, yourself and the situation, and note:

- What emotions are you experiencing?

- What body sensations do you notice?

Stay in the same position, and think about a recent work situation that you handled with great confidence and competence. Remember all the positive ways things worked out as you:

- Notice how you feel

- Notice your body sensations

What, if any, differences did you experience between the two activities?

When we notice we have negative thoughts, we can replace them with more calming, empowering ones in order to be more grounded and better positioned to shift our unproductive thinking at Step 4. I can remind myself about the common dynamics of triggering events (I'm just triggered right now...this too shall pass), focus on the positive (What can I learn and take away from this situation to help me in the future?), remember to trust the process (Everything happens for a reason), consider adjusting my approach (So that approach didn't seem to work...what else can I try?), and focus on the intent of others (They are doing the best they can and not trying to be difficult).

Go to the Appendix for additional resources about using these self-management tools.

PAUSE

In challenging situations, we can always hit the pause button! It is important to develop the habit of pausing when we are about to over-react. If we step back from the interaction and watch what is occurring in ourselves and among others, then we may get an insight into how to best move forward. From a place of reflection, I am more likely to ask a question that could benefit me in several ways. It gives me time to breathe and center myself and to gather more information. I may realize I misunderstood what the person was saying or realize there were other data I had overlooked when I initially felt triggered. Asking questions can also give me the time and space to use stress management tools or explore how I interpreted the situation and what was fueling my story.

Another tool to shift triggered reactions at Step 4 is to quiet your mind and become still. We can pause, clear our minds, and be in silence. Some may find it helpful to pray and surrender the situation to a Higher Power of their understanding. Often in these quiet moments, I receive helpful intuitive insights and feel more peaceful, centered, and clearer about what to do next.

UNMET NEEDS

At times, when I struggle to shift my negative thoughts at Step 4, I have found it useful to think about the possible reasons or intentions behind what the person said or did. I remember Marshall Rosenberg talking about a foundational premise of Nonviolent Communication (NVC) when he emphasized how people behave in ways that meet their unmet needs. For instance, during a meeting, if someone makes an offensive joke, they may be trying to meet their needs for belonging. Or if two people are having a side conversation, they may be meeting their needs for understanding or clarity. And if someone interrupts me, they may be trying to feel included or recognized for their ideas. While I may not appreciate someone's actions in the moment, it is useful to try to understand and relate to the possible underlying reasons for them. When I shift my focus away from my negative thoughts to think about the reasonable intent and unmet needs of the people whose behavior is the source of my trigger, I am more likely to feel greater empathy and enough distance to de-escalate my emotions to a level from which I can choose a productive response.

Go to the Appendix for a worksheet to practice identifying intentions and unmet needs fueling unproductive behaviors.

There is an old Cherokee story[2] of an Elder talking with his grandson about the battle that goes on inside of us. He said we all have two wolves fighting in us. One is peaceful, loving, compassionate, and kind. The other is full of anger, jealousy, greed, false pride, arrogance, and resentment. The young child asked, "Which one will win the fight?" And the grandfather replied, "Whichever one you feed." If we replay and obsess about negative thoughts and criticisms, we will strengthen them, and they will win. However, if we intentionally change these unproductive thoughts and focus on what is positive about a situation or at least possible, then as a result, we shift our emotions and are far more likely to respond effectively. It will all depend on our ability to choose positive, productive intentions at Step 5.

Chapter 6

STEP 5 — "CHOOSING" YOUR INTENTIONS

"That was the day she made herself the promise to live more from intention and less from habit".

~ AMY RUBIN FLETT

As Laura paused to move to the next slide of her presentation, Bill asked, "What are the sources of your data for that last statement?" She felt immediately irritated that he had interrupted her flow. As she felt her chest tighten and her jaw tense, she thought, "Why does he always ask questions that make me look unprepared? He always questions my competence!" Sounding frustrated she said, "I sent that information to everyone last week to review for this meeting." As she pulled up the next slide she noticed he looked frustrated and turned away. He seemed checked out for the rest of the presentation.

When she told me this story, I asked her what her intentions had been at that moment. She said she was just trying to focus everyone back on the presentation. As I asked her more questions, she realized that under her tone had been her intention to shut him down so he wouldn't interrupt her again. She then saw how her negative intention had fueled her unproductive reaction. Step 5 is one of the more unconscious steps in The Triggering Event Cycle. Based upon our interpretation at Step 3 and our additional thoughts at Step 4, we "choose" the motives that will influence our reaction. I say "choose" because most people seem completely unaware of this part of the process until they have used the activities in this section to increase their capacity to navigate Step 5 effectively.

Our actions follow our thoughts and intentions. Just like using a GPS, we set our destination with the intended outcomes of the action we are about to take. If we choose unproductive thoughts and intentions, we will most likely react in ways we later regret. If we choose productive, positive intentions, then our focus, energy, and actions move into alignment with them.

UNPRODUCTIVE INTENTIONS

Similar to the previous example, if I intend to put someone in their place, then my tone, facial features, stance, and words all seem to send that message and accomplish my intention. However, if instead I intend to honor their question and deepen understanding, then my body posture will most likely soften and open, my tone will ease, and the tempo and sharpness of my speech will slow down and shift. Positive intentions are like a compass that guides us along the more productive path.

When I am more aware of my common unproductive intentions, I am more likely to notice when I am about to react out of them in the moment. This split second of awareness can be enough for me to shift my thinking and choose more productive intentions. Some negative intentions that have fueled my past unproductive reactions, include: to be right and prove others wrong, to try to make people learn, to change their perspectives, to prove I am competent, to seek approval, to put others "in their place," and to avoid conflict and confrontation.

Think about a few times you have reacted less effectively during difficult conversations. In your journal, make a list of your less productive intentions at Step 5 and note how they may have fueled your reactions.

Go to the Appendix for a more extensive list of negative intentions.

PRODUCTIVE INTENTIONS

"There is nothing more potent than thought. Deed follows word and word follows thought. And where the thought is mighty and pure, the result is mighty and pure."

~ Gandhi

If we notice we feel triggered at Step 5, we can shift our negative intentions and refocus on more positive, productive outcomes. Some of the intentions that have helped me respond more effectively include: meet people where they are, do no harm, engage in respectful discussion, explore differences of opinion, deepen understanding, trust the process, and model the skills and concepts I am teaching.

Think back to some examples when you responded more effectively during difficult workplace situations. In your journal, note the productive, positive intentions you chose at Step 5. Then reflect, how did your various responses impact others? *Go to the Appendix for a more extensive list of positive, productive intentions.*

When we choose negative intentions, we are more likely to react in unproductive ways. Below is an example that shows how we can respond more effectively if we shift our negative intentions at Step 5.

A client, let's call her Briana, shared a common difficult situation she often experienced on Search Committees. When the Chair asked the members for feedback on the three finalists, one senior leader, Jerry, said, "I like Chad. And Kelly would be fine as well. But Tiana wouldn't be a good fit. Don't get me wrong, I think diversity is important, but we also don't want to lower our standards." She was enraged, especially when no one else countered his comments. Once again she was the only one who had the courage to speak up and confront these biased comments. Her first thought was to say something like, "This is another example of racist practices that keep our organization so white!" But she stopped herself knowing that this could be a CEM, a career-ending move! A couple of others offered their assessment of the candidates while she took a few deep breaths and thought through her options. She then said, "I want to ask us to slow down a moment. Before we make our recommendations, I'd like us to revisit the core competencies we identified for this position and then use these as we offer our feedback about each candidate. I actually liked all three of them on a personal level, but I think we will find some clear distinctions when we assess their demonstrated capacities against our envisioned outcomes." After a pause that seemed to last forever, the Chair agreed and they started to center the competencies in the conversation.

Initially, Briana wanted to call out her colleague on his racist comment and put everyone in the room on notice that she would not stand for similar behavior. She stopped herself when she anticipated that her approach, fueled by these intentions, would most likely damage her relationships with this colleague and the other members of the committee. In addition, she was concerned she might lose some credibility in the group and miss an opportunity to teach the group how to be effective in similar situations in the future. She decided to address the inappropriate comment in a way that furthered learning and refocused the conversation on competencies, not personal opinions and "likability." Her intent was also to model how to respectfully engage during a challenging situation while maintaining effective working relationships. When she responded, the group members readily focused on the core competencies, including the capacity to create inclusive work environments and effectively serve the increasingly racially diverse client populations. Her colleague was able to "save face" and actually participated in identifying a few competencies in the conversation. In the end, she believed they identified the most competent candidate.

Exercise

SHIFT NEGATIVE INTENTIONS

Think about a recent triggering situation in which you reacted unproductively. Make some notes in your journal using the following prompts:

1. What were the less productive, negative intentions you had in that moment?

2. How did you react less effectively? What was the impact of your reaction?

3. Rewrite these negative intentions into more productive ones.

4. If you had responded out of these new intentions, what would you have said and done differently? What might have been the impact of your response?

Next, in your journal, make a list of 4–5 of your more common unproductive intentions. Then, practice rewriting them into more positive intentions.

ANTICIPATE AND PREPARE

We can increase the likelihood we will respond effectively if we prepare for difficult situations. Just like an athlete improves their performance by visualizing success, we can anticipate potential triggers and practice effective responses. In your journal, write about the following:

- What is a situation in the near future in which you anticipate you could feel triggered?

- Write out the common unproductive intentions you have thought in similar situations.

- Rewrite these into more productive intentions.

- Imagine being in the situation and thinking about these more positive intentions.

- What body sensations do you notice? What are your emotions?

- What are 1–2 productive responses you might make? What do you envision the impact will be of your actions?

START WITH A POSITIVE INTENTION

I was on a project team and we were brainstorming possible ideas. A few members of the group got very excited about an idea that I thought was completely outside the scope of our project. I was getting very concerned that the "train had left the station" and more and more people were backing this idea. I wanted to get the conversation off of this tangent, so I started my comment by naming my intention in hopes that folks would pause and notice our dynamics: "I like the ideas we are discussing, but I am wondering if they are outside of our scope. Could we take a moment to revisit our charge?"

Reflect back on a difficult situation where you reacted less productively and imagine how you could have started your response by stating the positive intentions behind your comments. I have had good success with this technique, especially when I thought there might be some resistance to my ideas. I believe people appreciate the transparency of my intentions since they don't have to second-guess or figure out my motives.

SELF-MANAGEMENT TOOLS

When you notice you are about to react out of negative intentions, you can use some of the self-management tools from Step 4 and pause, breathe, and take a break from the conversation to complete the following:

- Write down the negative intentions you were thinking

- Then cross them out completely

- Write out more productive intentions

- Repeat these to yourself 4–5 times or write them out 4–5 times

Most of our negative intentions are like old ruts in a road. If we keep driving the same way, we end up stuck in the same rut. We need to practice and repeat these new, positive intentions over and over until they form new pathways for us to easily take. To create new positive tracks, add this practice to your morning routine:

- Imagine 3–4 activities you have planned for the day

- State aloud your positive intentions for each one or write them in your journal

- Repeat these intentions a few minutes before you start each of these activities

Just like using a GPS, we can intentionally set our course as Laura might have done if she had been able to shift her intentions at Step 5:

As Laura paused to move to the next slide of her presentation, Bill asked, "What are the sources of your data for that last statement?" She felt immediately irritated that he had interrupted her flow. As her chest tightened and her jaw tensed, she thought, "He does seem to always ask questions about my sources, though I doubt he is intentionally trying to trip me up. Maybe he didn't have a chance to review the prep materials I sent. I can answer him, and maybe others need this information as well." She took a deep breath and answered his question, "I appreciate your question. There are several key sources I want to highlight...." Once he seemed satisfied, she mentioned, "I know this is a busy time and my guess is folks didn't get a chance to review the materials I sent a few days ago. I will have them resent so they are in your inbox again this afternoon." He nodded as she pulled up the next slide.

When we successfully navigate Step 5, our positive intentions fuel productive responses. But what if you only have a couple of tools in your toolbox? In the next chapter, I outline a wide range of skills that have helped me react effectively at Step 6.

Chapter 7

STEP 6 — TOOLS TO RESPOND EFFECTIVELY

I used to believe that if I just learned enough tools or had enough experience then I could handle any difficult dialogue or triggering event. While both expanding my toolkit and deepening my experience are helpful, I have found the greatest way to prepare to respond during triggering events is to focus on *myself* as the key instrument of change. I am far more likely to choose a productive response at Step 6 if I have effectively navigated all of the previous Steps in The Triggering Event Cycle. The order in which I do them may not be as important so long as I use stress-releasing activities to de-escalate my emotions and physiological reactions and then revise my initial interpretation as well as any negative thoughts and intentions.

In the following section I revisit several of Kerry's triggering situations I outlined in the Introduction and identify ways she could have responded more effectively if she had used some of the tools at the different Steps of The Triggering Event Cycle.

As she is taking off her coat, Kerry sees a message from her boss, Karen, to come see her as soon as she gets in, and she is irritated all over again as well as stressed out about Karen's reaction. She stops this train of thought by remembering that other teams have submitted their reports late and that Karen can be reasonable at times. As she takes two more deep breaths, she repeats her favorite mantras several times, "All will work out in the end. This too shall pass." She takes a moment to plan how she wants to engage Karen as she walks to her office. With a smile she greets her boss, "Hey Karen, I want to apologize for not sending you the report yesterday. I know this has put you in a bind." After Karen gruffly replies, "I hope I don't come to regret giving you this assignment," Kerry takes another deep breath and says, "My next stop is to work closely with John and I believe I can get it to you by mid-day tomorrow. And I appreciate your giving me this opportunity. I already see how it has benefited some team members." She pauses to see if Karen would say anything else, and then continues, "And next week I'd like to do a 'Lessons Learned' meeting with the group and then debrief the whole process with you. Is there anything else you need me to do at this point?" When Karen says no, she thanks her and then leaves to stop by John's cubicle.

She anticipates he might still be frustrated with her as she says, "John, do you have a moment? I'd like to talk about the project. If not now, might we be able to gather within an hour?" John says he could meet then, so Kerry continues, "I first want to apologize for raising my voice with you yesterday. I was wrong to treat you that way. I know you are working on this project and juggling other priorities as well." She pauses to see if he wants to respond, *and when he doesn't she says, "I also want to see if you have any questions about what I need from you as well as to clarify the revised timeline. Is there anything else you need in order to send it to me by 3pm today?" Satisfied that he understood her message and didn't seem to need anything further, Kerry goes back to her desk to finish up the slide presentation for Friday, knowing that the project lead would ask about her progress at the next meeting. She is having trouble concentrating as she's replaying her conversation with Karen, so she decides to take a moment to make a quick appointment for a massage that weekend and take her mind off of work for a moment. Then, grabbing her water bottle, she reminds herself that she is doing the best she can with the people and resources she has and that there is nothing more she could do right now on the report. She does a few stretching exercises as she walks to the water cooler to re-center herself. Back at her desk, she pulls up the slides and takes a moment to read a few of her favorite motivational quotes on her bulletin board and imagines herself completing the slides and emailing them to the team.*

She is so focused on the presentation that she is now a few minutes late to the project meeting. Walking quickly to the meeting room, she pauses at the door to think about her intended outcomes for the meeting and the 3 key points she wants to report. As she enters, she catches the leader's eye to send a nonverbal apology, and then at the next pause in the conversation she apologizes to the group for being late.

She has a quick 15 minutes to eat lunch and think about her next meeting where she anticipates, as at the last two meetings, being interrupted by the men in the room. Unfortunately, she is right. After the first time someone speaks over her she pauses, listens to her colleague's point, then continues what she was saying with an even tone. The 2nd time she experiences a man interrupting her and challenging her point, she says, "I'd like to finish my comment, and I think I will have addressed your question. If not, I'll gladly discuss it then." She then glances at the team leader as she continues. A few minutes later she hears another man put forth a very similar idea to the one she had suggested earlier and all of the team now seems to want to move in that direction. When no one else notes how his idea is what she had said at the start of the meeting, Kerry takes a deep breath and says, "Rich, I like the idea, and it seems related to what I said earlier. To keep building, what if we…" After the meeting, she asks for some time with the project lead to talk about the group's progress. Her intention is to raise the pattern of gender dynamics she experienced and ask the leader for his ideas on how to address them so the group is more productive in the future.

Just as she sits back down in her office, John drops by and asks her what she thought of the final section he just sent her. Kerry looks at her computer to take a moment to adjust her facial expressions and remind herself that he is doing the best he can. She thanks him for getting it to her. She checks her tone as she tells him she has been in meetings since they last spoke but after a short phone call she will have about 20-minutes to look at it. She then asks if he will be around to meet with her after that.

As she looks over the section, she notes four areas that need reworking and emails John about them saying she would call in a few minutes to talk with him. She focuses on a few other emails to give him time and also to give herself a moment to ease her frustration, and then calls and they agree he would send her the final revision within an hour. She checks her watch and realizes that would still give her a few moments to give it a final review before sending it to her boss by end of day.

In a follow-up coaching session that week, I asked Kerry to identify all the tools she used to help her navigate this series of challenging situations. I think she was surprised by how many ways she had effectively implemented all of the skills we had practiced in our sessions. It can be very helpful to identify times in your own life when you responded effectively during difficult situations. Regularly reminding yourself of these tools and ways of engaging may increase the probability that you can choose to respond in similar ways in the future. Keep a list in your journal of all the ways you have responded productively in difficult situations, as well as the impact your response had on others. You may want to review this list before meetings or conversations you anticipate may become challenging.

BUILD YOUR TOOLKIT

I often wish I had an instruction manual that told me exactly how to respond to every type of triggering situation. There is no checklist or prescription that works every time, except maybe to be fully present, authentic, and intentionally respond to what is actually occurring in the moment for you and others. While there is no rulebook, I have found numerous tools and approaches that have helped me to engage during difficult situations. Which of these tools I choose depends on the context and complexities of each specific moment. Below are some of the tools I tend to use more frequently.

P.A.I.R.S.

Over the years, I have developed different acronyms to help me remember various skills. "PAIRS" is the most recent version that I use. The acronym stands for:

P ~ Pan

A ~ Ask

I ~ Interrupt

R ~ Relate

S ~ Share

I do not necessary use these tools in any set order, though I do tend to pan and ask questions initially to gather more information and get more centered in the moment.

P: PAN

PAN stands for Pay Attention Now. Just like a video camera takes a panoramic shot of a scene, we can "pan" or scan ourselves and the people in the environment in order to get a fuller, wider view of what is actually occurring. The first aspect is to pan and notice both what I am experiencing in my body as well as what is occurring around me. The next part is to consider if I want to share what I am panning with others. I deepened my understanding of this skill through the work of Elsie Y. Cross and Associates and their concept of "Tracking."

I was consulting in an organization and started to feel anxious as two of the organization's top leaders got into in a very contentious argument with each other during a meeting. My heart started racing and my breathing was very shallow. I felt tension and stress in my chest and was beginning to question if I could handle the situation. My initial story was I was over my head and not competent enough to help them move through this. I noticed how the voices of the two top leaders were louder than earlier in the conversation and each started talking before the other had completed their statement. Several other team members seemed to be looking at the ground or each other with frowns and raised eyebrows. The energy in the room had shifted to far greater tension and heaviness.

When I focused on observing or "panning" myself and the environment, I gathered more information that helped me diagnose what was occurring in the moment. Based on my assessment, I identified a variety of options to engage. I could *redirect* the conversation (I think we may be getting off the topic a bit; How does this relate to the agenda we were discussing?) or use a more *indirect* approach to productively move forward (I think this is a good time to take a break and we can revisit this when we come back). I also could choose a more *direct* response and one of these tools to describe what I was panning as a way to intervene and have the group members reflect on their process:

- I am noticing you each are speaking with more energy and volume than a few minutes ago. I am curious what is going on for you.

- I notice you both seem to start talking before the other has finished. I wonder if we can slow down to better understand what everyone is trying to communicate.

- I don't believe he was finished with his comment.

- I'm noticing the body language of people who are not engaged in this conversation right now.

If I decided that the group seemed to have the capacity to discuss their dynamics, I might then ask a question to involve more participants in the conversation, such as:

- I am curious how others are making meaning of what is occurring?

- How are these dynamics similar or different to what commonly happens in your meetings?

- What is the impact on you when top leaders engage in this level of disagreement?

Doing a "systems check" (see the related section in Chapter 5) is an example of panning myself. During a difficult situation, it is helpful to notice and observe the following as I am deciding how I want to respond:

- What am I feeling? (Step 4)

- How triggered am I on the -10 to +10 scale? (Step 4)

- What are my body sensations and physiological reactions? (Step 4)

- What was the stimulus, the trigger for me? (Step 1)

- How am I interpreting what I think is happening? (Step 3)

- What assumptions am I making? (Step 3)

- What additional data or information might I have overlooked initially? (Step 3)

- What are my initial negative thoughts (Step 4) and unproductive intentions (Step 5)?

- Why might I be triggered? What intrapersonal roots might be involved? (Step 2)

It is also important to pan the details of what is occurring around you. The challenge is to simply witness and observe without making any judgments, interpretations, or conclusions. It takes skill and practice to consistently distinguish between the stories and assumptions we create and the actual details and facts of what occurred. The following prompts help me focus on "just the facts" and remind me of some of the interpersonal dynamics to pay attention to as I pan the environment:

- How are people reacting nonverbally?

- How has the tone of the conversation shifted?

- Who is talking? Who is quiet?

- How much airtime do different people take up?

- Who has changed their way of engaging recently?

- Who is interrupting? Who gets interrupted?

- Who is looking at whom?

- Whose comments get addressed? Whose "plop" without comment?

- What issues are brought up? By whom?

- Whose ideas get considered? Whose don't?

To use what we pan as we respond requires a more complex, advance skill set. There are a number of tools we can use to share what we are panning in the moment, including:

- It seems some people were impacted by that statement, am I right?

- I'm noticing that some people get interrupted as they try to share... anyone else notice this?

- I noticed when we started talking about this, a number of people looked down or checked their phones... I'm curious what is going on for folks?

- You shifted in your chair and looked away from me as I was responding to you. I am wondering if you had a reaction to what I was saying.

- I noticed how quiet everyone got. I'm curious why...

- The energy seems to have shifted in the last couple of minutes. I am curious what folks are thinking and feeling.

There may be times when it is also useful to share what you are panning about yourself using tools such as:

- I notice I had a reaction to what you said.

- That's a trigger word/phrase for me...

- I need to stop for a moment and talk about what just happened. I'm feeling uncomfortable because...

- This may have more to do with me, but I'm feeling uneasy with what you said and I'd like to talk more about it.

I find that panning helps me to slow down, get more present, and notice what is actually occurring rather than reacting out of my stories and assumptions. If I decide to respond by sharing what I am panning, then the conversation may help people deepen their self-reflection, authenticity, and productivity.

A: ASK

A client shared this story with me: In our bi-weekly one-on-one, my supervisor told me one of my direct reports had complained to her saying I was too aggressive and direct. I was surprised since I hadn't heard anything close to this, so I asked, "Ok. So what did you say to them?" I felt irritated when she said she had just listened and thought she would bring it up in our next meeting. She should have asked if they had talked to me before coming to her and then sent them back to have a conversation with me. Then, I remembered a couple of recent encounters with some direct reports where I had to stand my ground more clearly than I usually do. I stopped myself from offering an explanation at that point, thinking she might judge me as being too direct in this moment as well. Instead, I decided to ask questions, including, "Can you tell me more about what they said? What have been your observations of me over the past six months? What, if any concerns, do you have? And, how do you think gender expectations might be playing into this feedback?" As we talked, I shared more about my recent experiences as well as my belief that women leaders are held to very different standards and often penalized when we are clear, direct, and hold people accountable. I then said I definitely want to consider feedback about the impact of my actions and would appreciate if in the future she would encourage people to come and talk with me directly. I explained that this would help us build clear communication, clarify expectations, and work together to address any misunderstandings. I shared that her support in directing team members back to me will help send a message that going around people is not a productive workplace practice.

STRATEGIC QUESTIONS FOR CHALLENGING SITUATIONS

I wish I would first pause every time to ask a few questions before I had a knee-jerk reaction. Asking questions gives me both the time to get more centered as well as the chance to gather more information that might shape my response. In the process, others may "hear themselves" and possibly reflect on what they have said, as well as the impact of their comments. Below are several types of questions I have found useful in addressing difficult situations, especially if I am feeling triggered.

If someone is strongly disagreeing with you, you could ask:

- Can you give an example?

- Can you give me some background on why you feel so strongly?

- Can you help me understand what you disagree with or find frustrating?

If you do not agree with someone's idea or opinion, you could ask:

- What are your intended outcomes for that idea?

- How might that play out if we go in this direction?

If you want to state your perspective after someone has disagreed with you, you can start with:

- I want to make sure I understand your point. You are saying that... How close am I in describing what you are concerned about?

- As I listen to you, a dilemma for me is....

- I believe/think _____. How is this similar or different for you?

If you believe someone said something inappropriate or offensive:

- Can you help me understand what you meant by that?

- You probably didn't notice what the impact of that comment was when you said...

If you sense that someone may have felt triggered by something you said, you could say:

- I'm wondering if what I said had an impact on you...

If a colleague is upset about something but not fully discussing it, you could ask:

- What's the most ____ (frustrating, embarrassing, anxiety producing, etc.) part about that situation?

- What are your key concerns about this?

If you want to expand the discussion to see if others will engage the difficult dynamics, you could say:

- I am curious what others are thinking....

- I appreciate what you're saying. Anyone have a different perspective or something else to add?

Go to the Appendix for an expanded list of the PAIRS tools.

I: INTERRUPT

While asking questions is almost always a useful approach, there may be times when it is important to interrupt unproductive dynamics in the moment. A client I'll call Steve shared this example with me:

In a budget meeting, we were brainstorming ways to increase efficiency and cost effectiveness in our area. As some of the newer employees offered possibilities, the person with the most seniority kept dismissing their ideas.

The third time that she rejected someone's suggestion, I interrupted the process and said, "I'm concerned we may lose some of these good ideas. What if we chart them all and then go back and discuss the pros and cons?" When she then dismissed my idea for how to proceed, I continued, "Well, having them all written down would help me in this process. Many of these ideas are from the newer staff and I believe having a fresh perspective may help us now. Maybe times have changed and some might work."

Most often, in my experience, leaders and team members overlook and avoid addressing inappropriate or dysfunctional interpersonal dynamics in the workplace. I relate to feeling nervous about directly discussing issues for fear of making things worse or having the conversation get out of control. However, there are times it may be important to interrupt the dynamics that are occurring in order to be more productive and to create a more inclusive work environment. Here is another example from a client:

I had just finished painting the big picture for our teams' report to the senior leadership team and introduced one of my direct reports, Yolanda, to present our initial findings. After a couple of minutes, I noticed that several of my colleagues were looking at their cell phones while she was talking. At the next natural pause, I interrupted and said, "Yolanda, this may be a good point to stop and see if anyone has any questions before we continue." I looked around and made direct eye contact with my colleagues as they looked up from their phones. If this dynamic had continued, I would have made a more pointed comment the next time.

In addition to panning and asking questions, the following tools may be useful ways to ask people to stop and shift the current dynamics:

- I'd like to try a different approach to this conversation.

- I'm going to interrupt and shift us to refocus on….

- I don't feel we are engaging according to our group norms.

- Let's take a breath…

- I hadn't finished my comment yet…

- I don't think that comment is appropriate or productive.

After you interrupt, it may be useful to offer an alternative way to proceed such as, "I think we'll be more productive if we talk directly about the issues and not make assumptions or negative comments about the people involved," or "I notice that there are some side conversations occurring. I'd like to hear people's reaction to the proposal."

Exercise

WORKING AGREEMENTS

In my experience, it is helpful for any intact group to discuss and negotiate Working Agreements to guide their discussions and conversations. This important group development process can provide a structure within which group members can raise issues and concerns more easily if they want to interrupt unproductive group dynamics. In addition, groups that operate within these norms can minimize the chance of people feeling triggered. Below is a list of Working Agreements I commonly use with clients in workshops and meetings. Review the following list and note any you want to review in the meetings you attend:

1. Engage in open and honest dialogue

2. Participate fully

3. Speak from personal experience

4. Listen respectfully; Seek to understand; Listen harder when you initially disagree

5. Share airtime; encourage others to participate

6. Be fully present

7. Be open to new and different perspectives

8. Assume good intent; explore the unintended impact of comments and behaviors

9. Take risks: lean into discomfort; Be Brave

10. Respect and maintain confidentiality

11. Notice and share what's happening in the group, in you

12. Recognize your triggers; Share if you feel triggered

13. Trust that through respectful dialogue we will deepen understanding and achieve our goals

R: RELATE

Barb hesitated to go talk to her supervisor after he used an offensive term related to people with disabilities in their morning meeting. But she had seen a couple of people look startled and impacted, so she decided to talk with him before their next leadership meeting. She started by saying, "I know you didn't intend this, but I think you may want to revisit your comment from this morning's meeting." When he looked surprised and asked what she was referring to, she reminded him of what he had said. He immediately said, "Oh, I didn't mean anything by it. That's just the term I heard growing up. I'd never say it in front of customers." Barb decided to "relate in" as a way to ease the tension and possibly increase the chance he would consider her perspective. So she said, "I relate. I heard that term and many others like it that no one told me were offensive back then. I actually have to catch myself sometimes or I might unconsciously use it, too. I did see a couple of people react when you used it, and I know it got my attention as well." He changed the topic and seemed to dismiss her input, but in the next meeting, he referred back to that moment and apologized for using the offensive term.

I have found "Relating" to be one of the most productive tools I can use during difficult situations. In the past, and still today, I have sometimes not reacted effectively when others have disagreed with me or seemed to resist what I was saying. I would assume an adversarial stance and push back or state my position more strongly which usually resulted in their digging in their heels. I have found it far more useful to move out of this "right/wrong" energy and, instead, initially explore how I can relate to the other person and their ideas. When I enter the conversation using some of the following tools before I offer a different perspective, I find that others tend to feel more acknowledged, respected, and open to considering my suggestion:

- I relate to what you're saying.

- I share some of your concerns as well.

- I agree that what you're saying could happen.

I also use Relating to shift my own triggered reactions. When I recognize I am judging someone or wanting to distance myself from them, I can ask myself the following questions to build more of a connection from which to engage:

- How am I just like this person? Or I used to be?

- When have I said or done something similarly?

- When might I say or do something like this in the future?

When I see myself in others and try to relate to those whose behavior is the source of my triggered reactions, I am more grounded and emotionally present. From this energetic place, I am far more likely to choose an effective response that aligns with my core values and positive intentions.

At other times when I am triggered, I may not be ready to engage the person directly. It can be useful to invite other members of the group to relate to what the person is saying using some of these tools:

- How do others relate to that comment?

- Who can relate?

- Who has a similar experience? Can you say more…?

- What you're saying seems to relate to what so-and-so just said…

These approaches not only give me more information and context but also the time and space to center myself using the tools from earlier Steps. If it seems useful, after relating in, I may offer additional information and possibly an alternative perspective for others to consider. I find that people are more open to my ideas once they feel heard and that I have seriously considered their points.

S: SHARE

Jamal was excited to talk with his manager, Alex, about the progress his team had been making. Since their meeting two weeks before when his leader had finally signed off on the plan, the team had moved quickly to research possibilities and was ready to sign a contract with the preferred vendor. As Jamal was updating his manager, Alex interrupted and said he had changed his mind and wanted to go in a different direction. Jamal was shocked and speechless at first. As his boss started to talk about his latest idea, Jamal took a moment to calm himself and decide his approach. When Alex paused to breathe, Jamal said, "I have to say I am surprised and a little shocked by this change of direction. I thought we had already worked through numerous options and had agreed to this at our last meeting." When Alex dismissively said, "Yes, but I think this will be better," Jamal continued, "Actually, that idea seems similar to what we discussed a while back. We have already spent an extra month coming up with the plan and I'd like to continue in this direction. I am proud of all the hard work of my team and I believe this would be a beneficial move for our organization."

"Share" is the final set of tools in PAIRS. I find that difficult situations can escalate when people are arguing about abstract thoughts and opinions. In these moments, I find more success when I use self-disclosure to share my personal experiences, thoughts, and feelings. A colleague told me about a time his manager was complaining about the lack of results from a new team leader. He asked a few questions to understand more of the context and then said, "You may remember when I first started in that role. I didn't know what I was doing! It took me at least a month to get my feet under me, and even longer to get a solid handle on how to get things done around here. Do you remember?" When his manager nodded with a slight smile, he continued, "You actually were a great help to me back then. You showed me the ropes without making me feel too incompetent. What if I check-in on her and see if I can be of any help?"

When I share more about myself and my experience, others seem to engage more effectively and the conversation may shift out of the "head space" and into a more connecting "heart space."

SHARE TO TURN THE TIDE

There are numerous ways we can use tools to Share during difficult situations, including:

If you want to connect by sharing a story or example from your own experience, you can say:

- I can relate. Just last week, I...

- I remember when I…

- This reminds me of when….

If you want to share the impact of someone's comments or behavior, you can say:

- I'd like to share the impact of your comment…

- I'm feeling uncomfortable with what you're saying…

- Here's what's going on for me as I hear you….

To invite others to share their feelings or the impact they are experiencing, you can say:

- How are others reacting or impacted by this?

- I'm noticing I'm feeling___, anyone else?

- I'm noticing I have some concerns. Anyone else?

For an expanded list of the PAIRS tools, go to the Appendix.

It takes great skill, presence, and self-confidence to effectively share in these ways during difficult situations. When we authentically share our feelings, reactions, and personal examples we may be better positioned to use triggering events as "teachable moments" where everyone can develop powerful insights from honestly panning and reflecting on what is occurring in the moment. I believe that the dynamics that occur during many difficult situations often mirror those we experience in other areas of our work. If we can slow down the conversation and honestly explore what is happening in the moment, then all involved may develop greater insight, knowledge, and skill to more effectively handle similar difficult situations and conflicts in other settings.

There is no prescription for the perfect time or place to respond after a triggering event. There have been times I felt it would be more useful to talk to an individual privately either at a break or afterwards. In a one-on-one setting they may be more likely to engage with less defensiveness and more willingness to consider the feedback. More often, I tend to choose to respond publicly so that everyone who was involved in the situation can hear my comment. In this way my actions may support those negatively impacted during the triggering event and open the door for productive dialogue and learning.

Exercise

APPLYING PAIRS TO A DIFFICULT SITUATION

Reflect back on a recent difficult situation as you review the sets of skills in this chapter. In your journal, write down 4-5 different tools that may have been more productive ways to respond in that moment.

Using PAIRS (Pan, Ask, Interrupt, Relate, and Share) has been incredibly productive for me over the years, yet there still may be difficult situations that are not easily resolved with these tools. In those cases, I've often suggested the group take a break to reflect and de-escalate the level of emotion by saying:

- I think it would be useful to table this conversation for a couple of days so we all have time to reflect on what has been said and explore other possibilities.

- I suggest we take a break and come back to this conversation after we each have some time to reflect on what has been said and what may still be unsaid.

In some situations, it may also be prudent to consult with human resources personnel or your supervisor to explore a wider range of options for resolution and response.

Whatever tools and approaches you choose at Step 6, it is most important that you first get clear about your intention for responding by asking yourself:

- What do I hope to accomplish in this moment?

- How can I respond in ways that leave others feeling respected? And the group moving towards our goals?

- How might I feel if someone said this or did this to me?

If we have successfully completed all of the first 6 Steps in The Triggering Event Cycle, then our response will most likely contribute to the group's effectiveness and productivity. However, if our reaction is ineffective or is a trigger for others, we can still try to find a useful resolution at Step 7.

Chapter 8

STEP 7 — THE IMPACT OF YOUR TRIGGERED REACTIONS

"We are dangerous when we are not conscious of our responsibility for how we behave, think and feel."

~ MARSHALL ROSENBERG, *NONVIOLENT COMMUNICATION: A LANGUAGE OF LIFE*

I was co-facilitating a diversity training session many years ago when I responded to a participant who had made a very sexist remark. I initially felt very good about my response until he said, "You cut me off at the knees!" I couldn't remember what I said to him because I was out of my body when I reacted. But I do remember feeling deeply disappointed that whatever I had done had felt so violent to him. My behavior had violated my core values of respect and leaving people whole. Today, I have the skills to re-engage effectively and to work to repair the damage, but at the time I just moved on.

A client I'll call Robert told me of his overreaction when his colleague, Lisa, showed up as the "know-it-all" in a meeting he was leading. As this colleague was once again telling others what to do and critiquing every idea that was proposed, as well as correcting his leadership approach, he felt very angry and impatient. The next time Lisa started to speak he just couldn't listen anymore and so he focused on his notes to figure out how to move the agenda forward. After a moment, he cut her off somewhat abruptly and refocused on the other participants. When she tried to come back into the conversation a few minutes later, Robert ignored her and kept addressing others in the room. Later that afternoon, one of the group members mentioned to him how much they actually agreed with Lisa's idea, but had noticed it didn't get much traction and that she had seemed shut down and withdrawn for most of the conversation. Robert realized he had not been paying attention and had missed Lisa's comment in the meeting.

If we effectively navigate the first 6 Steps of The Triggering Event Cycle, then our impact on others at Step 7 will most likely be productive and useful. However, when we react impulsively on automatic pilot, our actions more often have negative consequences for those around us and even for ourselves. In this case, the group lost an opportunity to explore a potentially innovative idea and, in the future, may not get the best effort from Lisa. If Robert had more effectively navigated his triggered reactions, he might have acknowledged her idea while also gathering several more from the group and then inviting folks to identify the advantages and possible downsides of all the ideas.

There are many ways we react ineffectively in difficult situations. If we are in the "fight" mode we might self-righteously argue, interrupt, or debate to make our point, dismiss and minimize the input of others, direct explosive emotions towards others, use sarcastic humor or belittling comments to "correct" or embarrass others, aggressively attack or berate the person with whom we disagree, or bully others into doing things our way. Out of the "flight" mode, we might get very defensive and guarded, ignore and avoid the issue or dynamic, frantically try to smooth over any conflict, or shut down and disengage from the conversation. If we "freeze," our less effective reactions include blanking out and forgetting what we had wanted to say, as well as being immobilized by our emotions and unable to respond.

When we react in these ways, our actions not only undermine productivity and creativity, they often can trigger others. And then their over-reactions may become another trigger for us, and The Triggering Event Cycle repeats. One helpful tool to interrupt this continuous loop of multiple triggers is to stop and ask ourselves, "Could I have done something earlier that may have triggered their reaction?"

A client I'll call Jen told me a story of how she felt caught off guard and defensive when a colleague, with very intense energy, directed a pointed, sarcastic comment at her. She felt angry and her initial thought was to pull away and disengage. Instead, she said, "I'm noticing your comment. Did I say or do something that was offensive or triggering for you?" Her colleague was a little taken aback at first but then said she hadn't appreciated how Jen had dismissed her earlier suggestion. Not fully remembering that situation, she asked the person to say more about their experience and realized as she listened that she had been somewhat flippant and dismissive of her colleague's idea. She then invited others to weigh in about the suggestion and the group had a productive conversation. Towards the end of the discussion, Jen acknowledged the impact of her earlier comment and apologized for her off-handed remark.

It takes constant practice and presence for me to stop and wonder if I my behavior might have been a trigger for others. I may not always name the dynamic as directly as Jen did, but if I hold it as a possibility, then I am often less reactive and more open to ask questions of the person whose behavior was my trigger. As a result, I often gain critical insights about myself, deepen understanding, and build more effective working relationships.

How we react in unproductive ways may become a new trigger for ourselves as well. I felt angry when a colleague made a racist remark, but I reacted in a way that was not at all effective. Instead of staying in the conversation and trying again, I started to obsess about my "mistake" and swirled in negative thoughts like, "You really blew it," "You're not as competent as you think," and "The people of color in the group have lost respect for you." I missed the next several minutes of the discussion and by the time I was able to refocus, the conversation had moved on and I couldn't find a way to circle back. The best I could do was to talk with some colleagues after the meeting and identify a couple of ways I could respond more effectively the next time this happened. Upon reflection, I wish I had been able to say something like, "I realize what I just said wasn't very effective. I wanted to do something to acknowledge the impact of your comment, but even now, I don't know what to say except I felt uncomfortable." If I had been able to do even this much, I trust that others would have offered their perspectives and we could have reached a productive resolution in the conversation.

Exercise

IDENTIFY YOUR COMMON LESS EFFECTIVE
REACTIONS

In your journal, list some of the common ways you have reacted in difficult situations that were unproductive. Then note the negative impact your behavior had on others as well as on yourself at Step 7 of The Triggering Event Cycle. Think about how you could have responded differently in those moments that would have been more useful and furthered organizational goals.

When I am feeling triggered, I am far less likely to notice (or care about) the impact my comments and actions have on others. However, it is critical that we deepen our capacity to stay present to ourselves while also observing and panning the group dynamics as we react. If we do not notice and effectively respond when our reactive comments negatively impact others, then the intensity of the conversation may escalate and spiral out of control.

RECOVERY SKILLS

I believe it takes great humility to effectively engage others when our behavior has had a negative impact on them. I often want to explain, defend, and justify my actions, often by blaming others for causing my reaction. It can be tempting to get into a tug-of-war over who said what first and who started the chain reaction of triggers. I have found it far more productive to, instead, take responsibility for the impact of my actions without demanding that others do the same. If done with sincerity, acknowledging and exploring our impact will help de-escalate the triggered energy in the room and open up a space for honest dialogue about the mismatch between the intent and the resulting impact. It may not ever matter that others do not reciprocate and take responsibility for their behaviors as well. Modeling recovery skills will leave a powerful impression, rebuild damaged relationships, and serve as an example for others to emulate in future situations.

You may remember the part of the story from the Introduction when Kerry became extremely angry when her colleague's coffee spilled on her blouse as she was rushing to a meeting. Later that night, as she was telling her friend about how she had thought her colleague was an "idiot" and gruffly reacted when she bumped into him, she realized that she needed to go talk with him. The next day she stopped by his office and asked, "Do you have a moment? I'd like to apologize for making you spill your coffee yesterday..." As he invited her to take a seat he said, "No worries, accidents happen." She continued, "Thank you for your grace, and I should have been paying attention to where I was going. And I particularly wish I had not had such an irritated tone with you. Plus, I owe you a replacement coffee!" He again said it was no problem, and they talked for a few more minutes about a joint project and she left on a positive note.

When I create another difficult situation with my triggered behavior at Step 7, it is a relief to know that I can go back and talk to others about my unproductive reaction. My negative impact doesn't have to be the end of the story. I can choose humility and courage as I revisit the incident with others and make amends for my actions.

In these situations, I wish I could just hit a reset button and erase what I did or turn back the clock and start again. Unfortunately, the only way out is through! If I notice behaviors that signal folks may feel triggered by my actions (angry frowns, eye rolls, head shakes, crossed arms, turning away, looking down, side conversations), I can slow down the conversation and ask questions like, "Did I just have an impact on you?" or "It seems something I said had an impact, am I right?" If I am still unclear, I can ask the person if they are open to sharing more about the impact of my behavior. Once we understand another's perspective, we can acknowledge the impact and apologize for our comment. It is also helpful to thank them for the feedback and talk about how we intend to change our behavior in the future.

Sometimes we may not have any negative intentions and others still feel triggered by our comments or actions. In a recent training session on equity and inclusion, I was passionately talking about my anger at the seemingly daily news reports of more and more people of color across gender identity being killed while interacting with police. As I moved people into small groups for the next activity, a participant came up to me and said she was so deeply triggered she had shut down when I said that. She thought about "checking out" for the rest of the session, but had committed to being honest in the workshop, and so she chose to speak up. I asked her if she was willing to have a conversation with me and the whole group and she agreed since there were several people sitting near her who were also triggered.

We stood in front of the room together and told the group what had happened. I thanked her for her courage and asked her to say more about the impact of my comment. She told the group that she had a blue ribbon tied around a tree in her yard to honor police officers and she felt that the media was victimizing the police. As I looked around I assumed that there were other people in the room who felt triggered by my comment as well as some who were now reacting to her strong stance.

I acknowledged her passion and apologized for the impact of my comment and said, "I wish I had shared more fully before. I believe that most police officers are committed, dedicated public servants who sometimes have to risk their lives in the line of duty. And, as I hear story after story of another death, I am outraged that a small minority of officers are abusing their power and breaking the law." She then said she agreed and felt so devastated for the loss of life and for the families of the people who have been killed. I am grateful we had the space to talk through this difficult situation and I believe the whole group benefitted from the experience.

In difficult situations, many people seem to hesitate, hold back, and stay silent — possibly out of fear of negatively impacting others. While it is useful to be mindful of the potential impact of our actions, we also cannot eliminate any chance of triggering others. We have to have faith that we can repair and mend relationships when we engage others with humility, openness to learning, and authentic regret. It is important that we accept the reality that what we say and do may be a trigger for others and, if that occurs, we can seriously consider their feedback and make amends as needed. At times, they may be reacting out of old wounds or from misunderstanding what we said. And other times, we may realize that our behavior was out of alignment with our core values or the organization's expectations and we have an opportunity to own our part and shift our behavior in the future.

Throughout our lives we will always encounter situations where others feel triggered by our actions. Our first instinct may be to retreat or try to smooth things over. Instead, it is important that we stay engaged and listen deeply to others in the moment. Recently, I have heard numerous examples of workplace conflicts where someone with strong emotion says something like, "What you said triggered me!" and the conversation stops abruptly. People shut down, disengage, and move away from each other. I can relate to being at cumulative impact and only being able to say something like, "I am so upset by what you said!" And sometimes, I may not have wanted to explore it any further for fear of experiencing additional triggers or micro-aggressions.

People who experience these types of comments may pull away because they are afraid they made an irrevocable mistake or will now be seen as a bad person. Some have told me that this dynamic of people saying, "You triggered me!" is evidence that people are misusing the concept of triggers. I believe these dynamics may actually signal progress that at least people are finally speaking their truth instead of stuffing their reactions or writing others off. However, we can't stop there. In these moments, especially if your behavior is being named as the source of the trigger, we need to move towards others and stay engaged in the conversation. Recently I was "called in" about the consequences of something I said, and, after a deep breath and a quick prayer, I asked, "Can you say more?" By leaning into the conversation instead of pulling away or shutting down we ended up having a powerful discussion that had many of us learn and connect at deeper levels. The positive benefits of staying engaged in these moments will yield significant, measurable benefits to the organization and the people involved, but only if we have the courage to stay present, be open, and honestly reflect on how our behaviors may have contributed to the difficult dynamics.

And, at times in which I have been the one expressing deep emotion, it has been so powerful when others have joined me in meaningful dialogue to explore their impact. Once I felt heard and understood, I was more inclined to take a closer look at why I felt so triggered in that moment. Because I didn't have to use my energy to fight or argue with them, I was more willing to go inside and figure out what intrapersonal roots had been retriggered. This way I could focus on identifying ways I could continue in my healing process, as well as honestly acknowledge how my behavior may also have contributed to complicating the difficult situation.

Exercise

EXPLORE POSSIBLE RECOVERY TOOLS

Reflect back on several ways you reacted when you felt triggered that had a negative impact on others. If you could have a "do-over," what recovery tools would have helped you make amends and repair the relationship? You may want to ask others for advice and coaching about the ways you can respond more effectively at Step 7.

We can't do this alone. We need the insights and coaching of others. It is critical that we consistently seek feedback and counsel from trusted mentors and peers so we deepen our capacity to effectively respond at Step 7 when our triggered reactions negatively impact others. Life is a constant learning journey. We make progress step by step. In the spirit of Dr. Maya Angelou:

"Do the best you can until you know better. Then when you know better, you do better."

~ Dr. Maya Angelou

And as we continually learn new skills and tools to respond effectively in difficult situations, it is also critical that we focus on ways to minimize the chances we will feel triggered in the future by prioritizing our self care and the healing of our intrapersonal roots.

Chapter 9

MAXIMIZE YOUR EFFECTIVENESS: FOCUS ON SELF-CARE AND HEALING PRACTICES

"No matter how long you have traveled in the wrong direction, you can turn around."

~ SIMPLE REMINDERS

See if you can relate to this client's story:

I wish I had just taken a moment before I answered his question. But when he first questioned my research and then said my project plan was inadequate, I couldn't help myself. I was so tired from finishing up the presentation at 3am and was still getting over the flu, so I didn't have it in me to pause, ask a question, and engage him more respectfully. I just snapped and, raising my voice, "put him in his place"! It took me months to rebuild that relationship and regain his trust and respect. As I look back, I realize that his question triggered a memory of the times this one professor would publicly critique my work and never give me any positive feedback. Once I unhooked these old memories from my experiences with my colleague and did some healing work to take the sting out of those past situations, I was not as triggered by him anymore. In fact, we are beginning to partner on a new project.

We lose so much of our time, energy, and organizational capital when we overreact and mismanage difficult situations. But there is hope. We can use the tools at each Step to decrease the intensity of our triggered reactions and even eliminate many of our hot buttons. In this chapter, you will review self-care practices that can help minimize your feeling triggered during difficult situations and then explore tools to deactivate the power of old issues and unresolved situations that fuel your triggered reactions.

SELF-CARE PRACTICES

So many clients and workshop participants tell me how exhausted and stressed out they are at work. And no wonder! We have been socialized to take care of everyone else, to put others' needs first, to do whatever it takes to fix, solve, and serve. And add to this the pressure and expectation to be available 24/7/365, both virtually and personally. We are rewarded, even promoted, for over-working, over-stressing, and overdoing. The level of expected performance has consistently risen year after year due to a myopic focus on short-term gains without regard for the devastating impact on the humanity of workers.

We each play a part in creating and maintaining these dynamics. Many of us believe we are only worthy if we work extremely hard for very long hours and that we have to always be doing more in the office, at home, and in the community. We have come to worship this culture of busyness and gain a sense of self worth by how over-worked and exhausted we are. We feel pressure to stay current with the relentless tsunami of information and connectedness on social media. It seems almost impossible to take a break and turn away from these insistent demands. We seem to come up with increasingly creative excuses for putting ourselves last on our "to-do list". Everything and everyone is always more important. There is never enough time to do it all. We fear the backlash when we imagine if we even try to talk about the need to slow down, take a break, or delegate some responsibilities. We feel guilty if we even think about changing our feverish patterns. Like a hamster on a wheel, the fast-paced, frenetic momentum has a life of its own and it feels very dangerous to try to jump off.

We believe in the illusion that we can keep up this pace just a little longer. But, each day, our life force drains away more and more. If we do not begin to take better care of ourselves we will continue to deplete our capacity to weather difficult situations and we will feel triggered much more frequently. It is crucial that we pay closer attention to the warning signs that our lives are out of balance and that we need to prioritize ourselves and our self-care. Do you wake-up obsessing and replaying yesterday's challenges over and over? Experience waves of self-doubt and anxiety? Do you have insomnia and feel exhausted from lack of sleep? Do you spend your time with family, friends, and colleagues complaining about people and situations? Feeling resentful towards others? Are you isolating yourself? Have you depleted your energy stores so much that you need caffeine and sugar just to function? Are you so wired at the end of the day that you use alcohol or prescription drugs so you can wind down and possibly sleep? Are you lethargic and fatigued much of the time? Like you are hung over from the constant rush of adrenalin in your body? Do you have more headaches or seem to catch colds and flu more easily? Have nagging aches and pains in your body? Have you lost your enthusiasm and passion for work? For how you live your life?

"If another can easily anger you it is because you are off-balance with yourself."

~ Scottie Waves

When we are off-center, we are far more easily triggered and if we do not change directions, we will react with increasing ineffectiveness. We must invest as much time and attention into ourselves as we do into our work, our friends and family, and our social/community life. We cannot operate at our highest capacity if we are running on fumes and burning our candle at both ends. We have to make ourselves a priority and constantly rebalance our life activities to refill our stores of energy and replenish our emotional shield. We can no longer be useful and of service to others if we are running on empty and burned out. And just like we need to bathe every day, we have to focus on our self-care daily so that we have the capacity to live, work, and serve to our full potential.

"Rest and self-care are important. When you take time to replenish your spirit, it allows you to serve others from the overflow. You cannot serve from an empty vessel."

~ Eleanor Brownn

One of the most common excuses I hear is, "I don't have time to take care of myself." A few months ago, I decided to keep a daily record of how I use my time. When I reviewed my notes from the week I was shocked to realize how much time I wasted on activities that did not add much value to my life, like watching TV, zoning out on Facebook, and completing low priority tasks so I could get the illusion of productivity. I also discovered that I am far more efficient and innovative in the hours after I workout. So I have found more time lately by going to bed earlier and working out in the mornings before I focus on top priority projects.

Exercise

IDENTIFY HOW YOU SPEND YOUR TIME

On a sheet of paper, draw a large circle and create a pie chart with 12 equally-spaced intersecting lines. Each space between the lines represents 2 hours of time. Near the edge of the paper make a list of all the common activities you do in a day. Next use different colors to fill in the spaces in the circle to represent how much time you spend in each activity. For instance, if you sleep for 8 hours, you would use one color to fill in four spaces and label that area "sleep." If you watch a couple of hours of TV at night, you would use a different color to fill in 1 space and label it "TV." After you completely fill in the circle, notice how you spend your time. Then, keep track of how you use your time over the next 1–2 weeks. As you review your notes, identify 2–3 changes that will help you find more time for self-care.

A well-balanced life is key to taking care of ourselves. While each person's schedule will likely differ due to personality, current life issues, and interests, it may be useful to ensure that you have enough time each day for the central elements of a healthy life, including work, play, fun, exercise, socializing, good food, rest and relaxation, joy, self-enrichment activities, and sleep. We all deserve meaningful work in our lives. When I am engaging in activities that feed my soul I am re-energized. But I have to make sure I get enough sleep on a regular basis to maintain my energy and stamina. Consistent exercise and movement can refuel our energy stores and release built-up stress and anxiety. Eating a healthy nutritional diet is central to our self-care. We are what we eat and a diet full of sugar, caffeine, alcohol, and other chemicals or pesticides will deplete us over time. Many believe that drinking 8-10 glasses of water to flush our system is a relatively easy way to create greater health in our lives. Getting enough rest and quiet time can help deflect and ease the external noise in our lives. Meditation, prayer, or other spiritual/religious practices can also be powerful tools for living on purpose and engaging others effectively.

It seems that as we grow older we take less time to play and have fun. Unstructured time and deep laughter are fabulous ways to re-center and refuel. Others find rejuvenation through hobbies or learning activities that enhance their energy and good spirits. Whether it's dancing, singing, art work, socializing, community service, coaching a child's sports team, or hanging out with family and friends, whatever it is that brings you joy and happiness, make sure you include more of it in your life.

There may be times when we need some additional support in order to lead healthy, meaningful lives. Seeking counseling, coaching, or participating in 12-step programs can provide significant insight and guidance during stressful and challenging times. Regularly attending to all of these proactive self-care strategies will help us effectively navigate current life issues and difficult situations, as well as minimize the chances that we will feel deeply triggered.

SET CLEAR BOUNDARIES

"Let today be the day you learn the grace of letting go and the power of moving on."

~ Steve Maraboli

I remember a time I received a blasting email from a work colleague, like one of those red envelopes that get delivered by the owls in Harry Potter books! This had happened before and I had tried to work through the issues with the person, to no avail. At that time, I had been clear about how I expected them to interact with me in the future and made a commitment to myself that I would not participate in this type of dysfunctional dynamic. As I began to review my colleague's email, I quickly realized how inappropriate it was and I deleted it without reading it. I decided if they needed something from me, they could write back in a much more respectful way.

Taking care of ourselves involves clarifying our needs and boundaries for what we want and what we will no longer tolerate. People will push up against the boundaries we create and if we have loose boundaries, they may violate them over and over again. But if we are willing to get clear and hold the line, then others either will learn to respect and work within our clear expectations or we may need to let go and walk away from people and situations that no longer serve us.

BUILD A COMMUNITY OF SUPPORT

Creating and nurturing a meaningful social support system can be an invaluable source of self-care. Reflect on the quality of your connections with friends, family and colleagues in your life. Do you have enough spaces where you can be your full self? Where you can exhale and breathe deeply? Where you can express yourself authentically and release? Are there people in your life that feed your soul? Who appreciate and celebrate you? Who deeply recognize your value and worth in the world?

Exercise

ASSESS YOUR SELF-CARE PRACTICES

In your journal, draw several continuum scales using a 0-10 rating: 0 = not at all and 10 = completely. Label the first scale "exercise," and place an "X" at the number that reflects how satisfied you are with the amount and quality of movement and exercise in your life. Create a scale for each of the following areas as you rate your current self-care practices: work life, healthy eating, sleep, time with family and friends, play, meditation, religious/spiritual practices, activities that add joy and happiness to your life, rest and relaxation, emotional care and release, stress management, activities that enrich your learning and creativity, ways to be of service, etc.

I wish I could say I am peaceful and centered all the time and that I never feel triggered! But I do notice that when I focus on my self-care, get enough sleep, am eating well, exercising, and paying attention to my thoughts, I am far less triggered and far more likely to coach myself out of any intense emotions before I react in ways that violate my core values.

THE BODY COMPASS

"You will know you made the right decision; you feel the stress leaving your body, your mind, your life."

~ Brigitte Nicole, *lessons learned in life*

I learned how to use "the body compass" as a way to access my inner knowing during my Life Coach Training program with Dr. Martha Beck. When I get quiet and tune into my body, I can use the sensations I feel to give me guidance. This tool is especially useful when I am trying to decide what I want to do. Once I have a sense of my body sensations that tell me "yes, do it!" or "no way!" then I can consider different activities and notice how my body reacts. Recently, I was asked to collaborate on an article and I was initially excited about the idea, but when I slowed down and tuned into my body, I felt anxious and stressed out. My chest was tight and I felt my energy drain away just thinking about the idea. In the past, I have ignored these messages and pushed through to accomplish tasks I thought I had to do or ones that others expected from me. The result, as you can predict, was I felt more exhausted and burned out in the end. Using the body compass to listen to ourselves in a deeper way can give us critical information to help us live a more balanced life of self-care. When we are a witnessing presence to our emotions and physical sensations, we can gain insights to guide our decisions.

"When I finally realized that I don't have to please every-one, I became free to be myself."

~ Katrina Mayer

Exercise

DAILY PRACTICE OF REFLECTION

Just like weeding a garden, we need to spend time each day reflecting on our actions, thoughts, feelings, assumptions, and attitudes and pull out those that no longer serve us or align with our core values. Each night we can identify those that deplete our energy and distract us from focusing on our top priorities as well as note ones that add value, result in positive outcomes, and bring us energy and joy. You may find it useful to complete morning journal entries to determine your positive intentions and goals for each day.

"The more you stay focused on your blessing the less stressed your life will be."

~ Jenni Young

Exercise

EXPRESS GRATITUDE

Another daily practice that yields immediate results is to intentionally identify what I am grateful for both when I wake up and just before I go to sleep. If I focus on gratitude, I set the tone for my day and find that I am more productive and engage far more positively with others. And, at those times when I may feel irritated or disappointed, I can balance my perspective by also recognizing what I value and appreciate in others or the situation. From this stance, I am far less likely to react ineffectively out of deeply triggered emotions.

"I have come to believe that caring for myself is not self-indulgent. Caring for myself is an act of survival."

~ Audre Lorde

I am recently getting over a cold that wiped me out for over a week. The thought of starting to exercise again or to create a more balanced life while I am trying to finish this book feels overwhelming! According to the laws of motion, it takes far more energy to start doing something than to keep it going. This has been my experience. I dreaded going to the gym this morning, but once I reached the 10-minute mark on the elliptical I felt like I could easily do another ten! And going again tomorrow feels more doable. Push through the inertia and start today to take better care of yourself. I suggest you set some goals in your journal and review them every few days. You might start with writing out a few declarative statements like, "I deserve to take care of myself," "I can only serve others if I have deep energy reserves," "I can put myself at the top of my to-do list so I can be more useful to others," and "There is enough time." Then, you can specify how you intend to take better care of your health and energy levels as well as how you plan to create a more reasonable and revitalizing work/life balance.

Feeling deeply triggered can be a wake-up call that indicates that something is out of balance in our life. In these moments, we may need to slow down, take a break, and check-in with ourselves to see what we need in our lives. It may also signal that we need to put far more emphasis on our self-care practices. We all need to be at our best if we are to create productive, inclusive work environments. There is far too much critical work and meaningful change that have to occur to create the world we envision for ourselves, our children, and our future generations. We all need to be healthy, centered, and fortified for the long haul.

TRIGGERS ARE A GIFT

"With everything that has happened to you, you can either feel sorry for yourself or treat what has happened as a gift. Everything is either an opportunity to grow or obstacle to keep you from growing. You get to choose."

~ Wayne Dyer

A client I'll call Teri told me about a meeting in which she felt deeply triggered when a couple of her team members were having a disruptive side conversation while she was discussing a recent policy revision. In a sharp, snarky tone she said something like, "Anything you two would like to add?" She immediately regretted her reaction as she noticed the rising tension in the room. As we discussed this in our session, I asked her to identify which of the seven intrapersonal roots may have been fueling her ineffective response. As we talked, she realized that she had felt anxious about the group's reaction to the policy change and was worried that she would have trouble supporting this policy since she didn't agree with it either. As we delved even deeper, she remembered a time at her former organization when she had been severely reprimanded for questioning her division leader about how a policy negatively impacted staff across gender and class. As she talked more about that situation, out of the blue, she remembered a painful memory of a time her mother had publicly disciplined her when she had disagreed with something she said.

At times, when our triggered reaction is out of proportion to the current circumstance, we have most likely reactivated old baggage and intrapersonal roots that we brought into the situation. In my experience, I continue to trigger myself in similar instances until I have completed enough healing work to decrease the power and sting of those old memories.

"I've come to trust not that events will always unfold exactly as I want, but that I will be fine either way. The challenges we face in life are always lessons that serve our soul's growth."

~ Marianne Williamson

A client was deeply distressed that she had again felt triggered into remembering her experience of sexual assault from over twenty years ago. She had spent significant time in individual therapy, support groups, and several types of body work and had felt that, while she never forgot the horrific experience, she had made peace with it and had moved on with her life. As we talked, her frustration eased as she shifted her interpretation of this flash of memory to be a sign that she was ready for another layer of inner work. I believe triggering events are amazing gifts that illuminate areas in our lives and our past that need further attention and healing. These moments can be a wake-up call that leads us to deeper self-awareness and growth.

"Painful as it may be, a significant emotional event can be the catalyst for choosing a direction that serves us more effectively. Look for the learning."

~ Louisa May Alcott

Our triggered experiences may be an opportunity to see something about ourselves we have been avoiding or overlooking. They may offer a chance to see something new about ourselves we hadn't recognized before. If we embrace the opportunity and lean into the triggering moment with a sense of curiosity and wonder, we can ask ourselves questions, like: "What am I supposed to be learning in this moment?" "What unresolved issues and old baggage am I still carrying around that am I ready to let go of and release?" and "What life lesson is here for me to learn?"

Exercise

TRIGGERS AS GIFTS

In your journal, reflect back on times you felt deeply triggered and identify the gifts you received from those experiences. Did you identify attitudes or behaviors that no longer serve you? Did you get a gentle nudge to do some more inner healing work and find greater freedom from old traumas? Did you gain insights and life lessons about how you want to be in your life? When I feel triggered, it has been helpful for me to repeat a mantra like, "I am open to the learning of this moment. I am willing to learn and grow." Take a moment to write out these statements or any others that could remind you to stay open to the lessons of the triggering event.

FOCUS ON HEALING

I am convinced we can heal ourselves enough to minimize the impact of most of our intrapersonal roots. As I continue to do healing work around my father and my experiences with other men, I now rarely, if ever, feel deeply triggered in the same ways I did when men would interrupt me or try to exert power over me. Now, I easily respond in productive ways. Today, we have more tools to engage and respond effectively than we did in the past. We don't have to react out of old habitual patterns and outmoded survival strategies. We can take back our life and respond differently than we did when we didn't have the skills or safety we needed. But we first have to heal and release old traumas. It takes courage to honestly explore the past and identify unfinished business and unhealed wounds. By using your current skills and wisdom, you can be free from the baggage you have carried for so long. Healing old unfinished business will help you complete these aspects of your past, learn from them, move on, and know you have minimized the possibility of feeling deeply triggered by similar situations in the future.

"Everything is falling together perfectly, even though it looks as if some things are falling apart. Trust in the process you are now experiencing."

~ Neale Donald Walsch

There are many effective ways to do healing work, including individual and group counseling, community support groups, working with a spiritual adviser or mentor, life coaching, executive coaching, Re-evaluation Counseling, 12-Step recovery programs, Nonviolent Communication workshops, energy and body work, meditation, yoga, and numerous others. Whatever path you choose, you deserve the space to heal the past, release old baggage, and rewrite your stories about what happened so you can be free today to apply the lessons to your life. I believe we each have an ethical responsibility to continuously do our inner healing work so that our old wounds and unfinished business no longer seep out and negatively impact others and undermine our effectiveness in the moment.

When my life is going well, I dread the thought of digging around in my intrapersonal roots and unresolved old wounds. I ignore the gentle whisper of an issue or a fear, and push through it because life is feeling pretty good at the moment and I don't want to "ruin it." However, when I am feeling good is exactly the right time to invest in some deeper healing work because I will have the strength, stamina and life balance to reflect on the past and identify new insights without getting stuck and spiraling into difficult, scary spaces. And remember that pulling weeds when they are small is much easier than when they have grown 3 feet tall and sent foot-long roots into the ground. Listen for the whispers, the mild irritations, and the minor worries as clues to deeper healing. Explore these and shift them when they are malleable, before they take deep root. Because unprocessed issues, pain, anger and resentment will ALWAYS surface, often when we least expect or want them to! So the proactive healing work we do when we are feeling good in our lives will reap significant benefits for us as we respond more effectively in difficult, challenging times.

Some clients tell me, "I am too old. I believe you should leave the past in the past!" I believe it is never too late to heal and to reclaim more joy and freedom in your life. We need to be gentle with ourselves in this healing process. Every insight, no matter how small, is important. Every step leads to the next one. We may have years of habitual patterns and old wounds to heal and release. But once we make the decision to invest in ourselves, we may find we can heal rather quickly and shift our unproductive, reflexive reactions with increasing ease.

Exercise

EXPLORE OLD WOUNDS

I have found it invaluable to make the time and find a safe space shortly after I feel deeply triggered to journal about my emotions and begin to explore the intrapersonal roots that fueled my reaction. As I noted in Chapter 3, you can ask yourself some questions, including: "Who does this person remind me of?" "What past situations seem similar to what I experienced recently?" and "What feels familiar about this situation?" As in an earlier example, it is important to not stop asking these questions after you find your first answer. Be willing to continue to explore deeper down the root to see what older, unresolved issues may also be fueling your reaction. Over time, it can be useful to look back and read what you have written and add any insights and reflections as you review your entries. Writing about triggering events in this way is a powerful reminder that triggers are a gift, a valuable teacher, and a path to healing and liberation.

RELEASE YOUR EMOTIONS

You can also gain insights from being present as you express and release your emotions in a safe, comfortable place. I remember feeling deeply triggered watching the movie "Rangoon." I started to unexpectedly sob at one scene and so went into the spare bedroom and stretched out to cry and release my emotions. I had no idea why I felt so upset. After a few moments I saw a flash of my mother in my mind and started to cry even harder. She had died a couple years before and somehow I had triggered deep grief by watching the movie. To this day, I don't see a direct connection, though I am deeply grateful for that opportunity to grieve some more for the death of my mother. Afterwards, I felt such love for her and deep appreciation for all she gave me. Some people use a similar practice of making space whenever deep feelings arise, while others access their feelings and find release through dance, drawing, music, writing poetry, or other avenues. However you choose to create this sacred space, you deserve to always find ways to safely experience and release your triggered emotions.

I am so grateful to have a community of friends and a life partner with whom I can explore triggering situations and honestly express my emotions. I hope you cultivate a group of people who can be a witnessing presence and support you in your healing journey.

Exercise

YOUR PLAN FOR HEALING OLD WOUNDS AND OTHER INTRAPERSONAL ROOTS

In your journal, make a plan for how you will take the next steps, with others and by yourself, to resolve unfinished business and heal old wounds. You deserve to create this space! You deserve to be free!

If you create and follow a lifelong practice of self-care and inner healing, I know you will experience meaningful results. You will notice you are more centered and effective in your daily activities and you will feel triggered far less often. You may even find you laugh and smile more knowing you have all you need to make productive, intentional choices as you thrive in difficult situations.

Chapter 10

WE ALWAYS HAVE A CHOICE

"Between stimulus and response there is a space. In that space is our power to choose our response. In our response lies our growth and our freedom."

~ VIKTOR FRANKL

I was under a deadline and about to call the person in IT who was supposedly helping me. We had already exchanged several emails and they still hadn't fixed the problem. I was irritated and stressed out because I could not miss this deadline. As I started to pick up the phone, I saw a card posted on my bulletin board that read, "PAUSE!" I am so grateful I listened to that message or who knows what I might have said on that call! I took a couple deep breaths and noticed the negative thoughts I kept replaying, "This problem should have been fixed days ago! They better be able to help me right now! How incompetent can they be?" As I breathed again, I saw two other notes posted in front of me, "It all works out in the end" and "It's never too late to be what you might have been." I am so grateful I had the presence of mind to stop myself in the moment and use some of the tools from The Steps to shift my story and turn the tide. I felt so much more centered after repeating my new interpretations, "They are doing the best they can. Maybe this is a far more complicated problem than I think it is. If I am calm and grateful for their efforts, it may help them be less anxious and better able to help me." I imagined the problem completely solved as I called to ask if they needed anything further from me at this point. I was respectful, understanding, and actually, rather delightful! Funny thing, they had the solution to me by the end of the day. These tools saved me hours of stressing and obsessing!

I hope you realize you are not alone. It is very common to feel intense emotions during difficult workplace situations. And some particular colleagues seem to give us endless opportunities to practice these skills! It's not something to be ashamed of or an indicator of incompetence. Triggering events are not problematic in themselves; however, how we react can result in misunderstanding, escalating conflict, unproductive interactions, and resentment. The goal is not to stuff our feelings or never feel triggered, but, instead, to develop the capacity and the toolkit to intentionally choose how we respond in every moment. To turn off the automatic pilot and be thoughtful, not thoughtless. In difficult situations, others may act unprofessionally around us, but we can use the tools in The Triggering Event Cycle to respond with the respect, confidence, and clarity that meet our needs and help the organization move forward. As Victor Frankl reminds us, there is this space between the stimulus and our reaction where we have a choice. We have the power to choose how we will respond and what impact we intend to have on others.

And if at times we react unproductively in difficult situations, we can always begin again. We can acknowledge our impact and work to rebuild relationships. I believe that well-facilitated difficult conversations can provide powerful benefits in the workplace, including opportunities to clear up miscommunication, accelerate understanding of differing perspectives, build more effective relationships, and identify innovative solutions to complex problems. Authentic, engaged discussions ignite productivity, increase clarity, and mobilize team effectiveness.

At the same time, triggering events have given me amazing opportunities to learn and grow as a person and as a leader. When I shift my focus away from obsessing about others to examining my own reactions and intrapersonal roots, I find a treasure chest of insights and opportunities for further growth, healing, and skill development. Over time, I have developed a far greater capacity to stay present during difficult situations and intentionally respond in ways that align with my core values and further organizational goals. I have come to believe that it is not the situation, per se, that is the issue, but my reaction to it that holds the keys to greater effectiveness and my freedom. Today, I am far less triggered than I used to be and I more effectively facilitate difficult conversations when others are experiencing intense emotions.

I hope you discovered a wide variety of tools, concepts, and ways of being that help you anticipate, prepare for, and effectively navigate the intrapersonal and interpersonal dynamics you experience during difficult workplace situations. There is a Quaker saying, "Let your life be your teaching." I believe what we "teach" as we react in triggering events may have a far greater impact on others than most anything else we do as leaders. If you work with others, particularly in a developmental or supervisory capacity, I believe we have an ethical responsibility to continually deepen our competencies and self-awareness to effectively navigate triggering events so we model the skills and values we espouse.

I hope you track and celebrate your progress and success. Make a personal commitment to yourself to prioritize your development. Continue to deepen your awareness of your common triggers and implement a self-care and healing practice to explore and resolve your intrapersonal roots. Create opportunities for work teams and committees to talk about triggering situations and learn ways to effectively navigate through conflict and disagreement. Pay greater attention to the impact of your comments and actions and, if necessary, apologize as you rebuild relationships. And, maybe most important, be patient with yourself when you feel triggered. It may take a lot of practice before you readily use these tools in everyday work experiences. And if you occasionally make a mistake, remember you can learn as much from your ineffective reactions as when you respond productively. And you can always go back and make amends for the impact of your actions.

I want you to be the most powerful and effective instrument of leadership and change you can be. I want you to make a significant difference in your life and leave a legacy that continues to help others for generations to come. I believe the tools in this book are critical to our ability to achieve these goals and to show up as our best selves each and every moment. And the next time you are in a difficult situation, I hope you pause to use these skills so you can say "yes" to this powerful question from Allan Lokos,

"Am I about to speak and act as the person I want to be?"

Please visit my website to download copies of the worksheets in the Appendix, www.drkathyobear.com/book-worksheets.

And I would love to hear from you! You can *contact me* https://drkathyobear.com/contact to share your top three take-aways from the book as well as more examples of difficult, triggering situations!

I look forward to our paths crossing again in the future.

THANK YOU

Thank you for reading my book! I hope you found a treasure chest of tools and skills that you will dig around in for years to come! To show my appreciation, I want to give you access to my *10-minute, animated Training Video* that describes the dynamics of triggering events, as well as a *Companion Discussion Guide* to help you lead "Lunch & Learn" sessions in your organization. Visit **www.drkathyobear.com/book-gift** to access these resources.

To schedule a **free 30-minute strategy session** to explore the possibility of our working together, use this link, **www.drkathyobear.com/complimentary-session**.

For information about **working with me as an Executive Coach or Life Coach,** as well as upcoming webinars and in-person training events, visit my website, www.drkathyobear.com or contact me directly **www.drkathyobear.com/contact**.

ENDNOTES

[1] I first saw a similar continuum in the Life Coach Training Program with Dr. Martha Beck. She uses a scale in her tool The Body Compass. http://marthabeck.com

[2] Source: http://www.nanticokeindians.org/tale_of_two_wolves.cfm

ADDITIONAL RESOURCES

Beck, M. (2001). *Finding your own north star: Claiming the life you were meant to live*. NY, NY: Three Rivers Press.

Beck, M. (2008). *Steering by starlight: The science and magic of finding your destiny*. NY, NY: Rodale.

Brown, B. (2012). *Daring greatly*. NY, NY: Random House.

Brown, B. (2015). *Rising strong*. NY, NY: Spiegel & Grau.

Brown, B. (2010). *The gifts of imperfection*. MN: Hazelden.

Castillo, B. (2006). *If I am so smart, why can't I lose weight? Tools to get it done!* BookSurge Publishing.

Gill, R., Leu, L., & Morin, J. (2009). *NVC Toolkit*. BookSurge Publishing.

Obear, K. (2013). Navigating triggering events: Critical competencies for social justice educators. In L. M. Landreman (Ed.), *The Art of Effective Facilitation: Reflections from Social Justice Educators*. Sterling, Virginia: Stylus.

Rosenberg, M. (2005). *Nonviolent Communication: A language of life*. Encinitas, CA: Puddle Dancer Press.

APPENDIX

You can download copies of these Worksheets on my website

~ www.drkathyobear.com/book-worksheets

FURTHER CONSEQUENCES OF MISMANAGED DIFFICULT SITUATIONS

Directions: As you review the following, check (☑) which of these seem familiar to you in your current work environment.

○ There is much more tension, stress, discomfort and conflict in the workplace

○ Our work relationships are damaged, possibly beyond repair

○ We end up over-working to complete projects when others refuse to work with us or passive-aggressively "forget" to complete assignments on time

○ Peers and supervisors don't trust us or depend on us as much

○ We are left out of the loop and not included in important discussions and meetings

○ Others hold grudges towards us and gossip in ways that may damage our reputation

○ We are often misunderstood and misinterpreted

○ We keep obsessing about the difficult dynamics and miss what's going on around us in the present moment

○ Team dynamics feel more competitive than collegial

○ There is far more debating as people try to win arguments rather than find creative solutions to workplace dilemmas

○ We often feel guilty or ashamed for how we reacted

○ We waste a lot of time and energy in follow-up meetings and workplace gossip

○ We feel depleted, exhausted, alone, and isolated

Step 1:
Identify Your
Common Hot Buttons

Directions: Below is a list of some of the difficult workplace situations people have shared with me over the years. As you read each one, consider how much of an emotional reaction you would most likely have in that situation. Use the following -10 to +10 scale to rate each item.

(–) Negative Triggered Emotions	Positive Triggered Emotions **(+)**

10	9	8	7	6	5	4	3	2	1	0	1	2	3	4	5	6	7	8	9	10

| **High** | **Moderate** | Mild | Mild | **Moderate** | **High** |

A **When someone (colleague, direct report, supervisor, client, etc.):**

➤ Doesn't do what you ask or follow your instructions ⬭

➤ Doesn't acknowledge or respect your leadership ⬭

➤ Takes over as you are leading a meeting or making a presentation ⬭

➤ Doesn't follow through on what they said they would do ⬭

➤ Produces low-quality work ⬭

➤ Keeps making the same mistakes ⬭

➤ Is not very competent at their job ⬭

➤ Takes advantage of you ⬭

➤ Takes your idea and presents it as their own ⬭

➤ Takes credit for your work ⬭

➤ Keeps you out of the loop or excludes you from important conversations ⬭

- ➤ Lies to you ☐
- ➤ Engages in side conversations during meetings ☐
- ➤ Is on their computer or cell phone during meetings when you are talking to them ☐
- ➤ Gets distracted when they are talking to you ☐
- ➤ Goes behind your back to undermine you ☐
- ➤ Gossips about you ☐
- ➤ Gets angry about what you said or did ☐
- ➤ Is moving too slowly, slowing down your agenda ☐
- ➤ Tries to derail the planned approach or agenda ☐
- ➤ Is late and keeps you waiting ☐
- ➤ Interrupts you or others ☐
- ➤ Ignores your ideas ☐
- ➤ Cuts off the conversation before you have a chance to express your thoughts ☐
- ➤ Loves an idea only after someone else suggests something very similar to what you had recently said ☐
- ➤ Dismisses your ideas ☐
- ➤ Rephrases or rewords your comments ☐
- ➤ "Corrects" you in public ☐
- ➤ Is belittling or demeaning ☐
- ➤ Is controlling ☐
- ➤ Dominates the air time ☐
- ➤ Continually brings the conversation back to their ideas and opinions ☐
- ➤ Will not consider your input and thoughts ☐

- ➤ Keeps pushing their point ⬭
- ➤ Is unwilling to listen to others ⬭
- ➤ Has a very blunt or impersonal style ⬭
- ➤ Has an aggressive or forceful style ⬭
- ➤ Disrupts the conversation with "jokes," inappropriate laughter ⬭
- ➤ Makes snide, sarcastic, or passive aggressive comments ⬭
- ➤ Is arrogant or self-righteous ⬭
- ➤ Is patronizing or condescending ⬭
- ➤ Makes an insensitive or offensive comment ⬭
- ➤ Raises their voice to try to silence you or others ⬭
- ➤ Demonstrates bullying or threatening behavior ⬭
- ➤ Wants others to calm down, just "get over it," and move on ⬭
- ➤ Accuses others of complaining when they raise concerns about exclusion or what is not working well ⬭
- ➤ Only focuses on how much progress has been made, rather than on how much more needs to change ⬭
- ➤ Shuts down and withdraws if you try to confront them ⬭
- ➤ Is "set in their ways" and unwilling to shift their perspective ⬭
- ➤ Pressures you or others to assimilate, fit in, and "not rock the boat" ⬭
- ➤ Mistakenly assumes someone else is the leader when you are ⬭
- ➤ Gives excuses or PLEs (Perfectly Logical Explanations) for disrespectful comments and behaviors ⬭
- ➤ Rationalizes away disrespectful and inappropriate treatment of others as individual incidents or the result of something the target of the behavior did or failed to do ⬭
- ➤ Defends others whose behavior is disrespectful and offensive ⬭

- ➤ Colludes and "goes along to get along"
- ➤ Will only focus on their "good intent," and not the impact of their behavior
- ➤ Is only focused on themselves as a "good person" and refuses to acknowledge the cumulative impact of their repeated negative behaviors
- ➤ Refuses to consider feedback from you or others
- ➤ Debates and disagrees with everything you say
- ➤ Believes they are always right
- ➤ Pouts if they don't get their way
- ➤ Challenges the validity of the information or statistics being presented
- ➤ Criticizes your style or approach
- ➤ Never gives any positive or appreciative feedback
- ➤ Questions your competency or that of others
- ➤ Gives unsolicited coaching or advice on how you should act, think, or feel
- ➤ Only appreciates and acknowledges other people's work, not yours
- ➤ Is given a prime opportunity to advance but you are not, even though you have far more experience and competence
- ➤ Doesn't volunteer for difficult team assignments and you end up doing all the work
- ➤ Does something unethical or dishonest
- ➤ Is talking loudly in an impromptu meeting outside your office or cubicle
- ➤ Introduces your peers with their titles or degrees, and introduces you by your first name
- ➤ Sends you a blasting, critical email and copies your supervisor
- ➤ Is more concerned with protecting their "turf" than achieving the overall goals

➤ Is angry with you

➤ Is only concerned with "moving up the ladder" and "looking good" to the leader

➤ Gives you a challenging "stretch" assignment (something "positive" can still be triggering)

(c) When you

➤ Make a mistake or an error

➤ Do or say something inappropriate or offensive

➤ Do not know the answer to a question

➤ Don't know what to say or do next

➤ Don't have a solution to a problem

➤ Can't figure out how to effectively respond in a difficult situation

➤ Believe the conversation is about to "get out of control"

➤ Are the only person to bring up controversial issues

➤ Have a strong opinion and no one else agrees with you

➤ Get promoted to an exciting new position (something "positive" can still be triggering)

kathy obear
LIFE COACH
choose courage, speak your truth, live on purpose.

STEP 2:
IDENTIFY UNRESOLVED ISSUES AND OLD WOUNDS

Directions: Recognizing how our current reactions may be powered by unresolved old wounds and unfinished business can help us to differentiate between the retriggered roots and what is actually occurring in the present moment. Take some time to create a quiet comfortable, supportive, and safe space for yourself. When you feel centered and present, think about a time you felt deeply triggered and reflect on the following questions:

Does this situation remind me of one or more past experiences?

Do any specific people from my past come to mind as I think about this current incident?

The following prompts may be helpful when you identify an old issue or situation that feels connected to a current trigger:

Write out the details of the old situation. (Choose a format that you are confident will be secure and confidential.)

Who was involved?

✎ ....

....

What happened?

✎ ....

....

How did you feel?

✎ ....

....

How did you react?

✎ ....

....

Did anyone speak up or try to help/support you?

✎ ....

....

How were you impacted by this situation?

✎ ....

....

As specifically as you can, write out what you now wish you had said or done in that situation.

🖊 ....

....

....

....

....

....

Write about what you wish someone else had done to interrupt the situation and/or support you in the process.

🖊 ....

....

....

....

....

....

Then write out what you would like to say to this person(s) now if you had the opportunity (I am not recommending you confront them, just that you reclaim your voice and personal power.)

🖊 ....

....

....

....

....

What feelings are coming up for you as you reflect and write about this situation? (Give yourself the gift of release and express these feelings fully ~ to a trusted friend or counselor; through art; as you go running; or by yourself in a safe, comfortable space.)

After you have identified and expressed your feelings, you may gain some deeper insights into the situation and yourself. It may be helpful to collect these in a journal or below.

Step 2:
Identify Your Fears

Directions: Review each fear below and check-off (☑) all that feel familiar to you. Add any additional ones:

○ My personal issues will become the focus of the conversation: all eyes will be on me.

○ I will lose credibility

○ If I cry and show emotion, people will think less of me....

○ I won't be able to manage the situation.

○ The conversation will "get out of control."

○ I won't know enough.

○ If I challenge, I will be alone without any support.

○ I won't be able to express myself clearly; I'll be misunderstood.

○ If I am too confrontational or angry, then people will judge me, be mad at me, reject me, ostracize me, etc.

○ I will be seen as incompetent and "not good enough."

○ I'll let people down.

○ People won't like me or approve of me.

○ Things won't change.

○ I will make a mistake and be wrong.

○ People will be disappointed in me.

○ If I don't handle this well, people could be hurt.

○ Things will be worse off than before.

○ ....

○ ....

○ ....

○ ....

Next, reflect on how you reacted in a recent difficult situation that you think may have been fueled by some of your fears. Review the lists of fears as you write about the following:

What fears and anxieties might you have brought into this situation?

🖉 ....

....

....

....

....

....

....

....

....

What fears and anxieties may have been restimulated by the triggering situation?

How did you react based on these fears and anxieties?

kathy obear
LIFE COACH
choose courage. speak your truth. live on purpose

STEP 2:
IDENTIFY YOUR
EGO-DRIVEN DESIRES

Directions: Think about a difficult workplace situation when you reacted less effectively.

Which of the following ego-driven desires feel familiar and might have been some of the intrapersonal roots that influenced both why you felt triggered and how you reacted?

Power and control

- To be in control
- To reassert or regain power and authority
- To win the argument at all costs
- To prove others wrong
- To get my way
- To make people change and learn
- To make others do as I think they should
- To gain certainty and predictability

Status and approval

- To be right
- To prove I am competent
- To be perfect
- To be seen as the expert
- To gain prestige and status
- To gain the approval of others
- To look good, competent, or acceptable

Belonging and admiration

- To be liked at all costs
- To be admired and revered by others
- To avoid disgrace by any means necessary
- To create harmony and avoid dissatisfaction at all costs
- To keep people happy all the time
- To fit in and belong at all costs
- To be seen as one of the "in group," the "chosen one"

Think back to a recent difficult situation as you review the list of ego-driven desires:

Which of these ego-driven desires might have fueled your reaction?

What was the probable impact on others?

kathy obear
LIFE COACH
choose courage, speak your truth, live on purpose

Step 2:
Interrupt Assumptions, Stereotypes, or Bias

Directions: It is critical that we continually examine our thoughts for any beliefs or assumptions that may be grounded in biases or stereotypes. When we find some bias it is important that we interrupt our thoughts and shift our thinking to more closely align with the facts of the situation.

The following are examples of biases, stereotypes, and assumptions that could influence our triggered reactions in the workplace. Check which (☑), if any, seem familiar to you:

○ Older employees are resistant to change.

○ Younger employees are brash and do not respect authority.

○ New employees are green and "wet behind the ears."

○ Female managers are aggressive and demanding.

○ Male managers are domineering and part of the "old boy's network."

○ Staff of color have a chip on their shoulders.

○ White staff only care about getting ahead.

○ Very quiet people are not as productive or creative.

○ Very talkative staff are usually just out for themselves.

Think back to a triggering event and examine your thoughts for any assumptions, stereotypes, or unconscious bias. Write them in the left-hand column below. Then rewrite any assumption/bias to more accurately reflect the facts of the situation.

Assumption, stereotype, or bias	More accurate perspective
Example: New employees rarely have anything useful to add until they have been here 2 or more years.	While new employees may not be grounded in our organizational culture, they bring with them new, innovative perspectives and ideas.

kathy obear
LIFE COACH
choose courage speak your truth live on purpose.

Step 2:
Expectations
and "Shoulds"

The second aspect of the 7th intrapersonal root involves the types of "shoulds" and expectations we place on ourselves and others. When I am strongly attached to what I think others should or should not do or say, or if I have a rigid expectation that I want met, I have most likely set myself up to feel triggered into disappointment and frustration.

Instead of clinging so tightly to shoulds and expectations, it is more helpful to stay fully present in the moment and respond to what is actually occurring: to respond to what is, instead of pushing or trying to force what we think should be. The ability to "go with the flow" and respond to what is actually happening is a critical competency for effectiveness.

Directions: It can be insightful to develop a list of our innermost beliefs, convictions, rules, stances, and shoulds and then explore where and when we first heard them. Check (☑) any of the following that resonate with you:

◯ Don't make waves

◯ Don't rock the boat

◯ Leaders have to be calm and control their feelings

◯ It is unacceptable to make a mistake

◯ Leaders have to know the right answers

◯ Leaders should meet the needs of their employees

◯ Boys don't cry

○ Don't air dirty laundry

○ People should always to kind and thoughtful

○ You have to fight for what you want

○ Never ask for help; just do it yourself

○ It's not ladylike to be assertive and state what you want

○ You should never interrupt someone

○ Don't raise your voice

○ Always dress and act in a professional manner

○ Smart people are logical and analytical

○ Everyone should always get along

○ Everyone should always be included in decisions that impact them

kathy obear
LIFE COACH
choose courage. speak your truth. live on purpose.

STEP 2:
SHIFT YOUR "SHOULDS"

Directions: Instead of adhering to fixed shoulds and expectations, it is helpful to shift them to be less righteous and absolute. Below, make a list of 3-4 of your common shoulds and expectations of others or yourself. Then next to each of these, rewrite them into more of a preference or desire.

"Should" or Expectation	Preference or Desire
Example: Everyone should wait their turn and not interrupt others.	While I prefer not to be interrupted, if someone feels so passionately about an issue that they talk over me, I can listen to their point and then tie it into mine as I finish sharing my thoughts.

Reread each of these shoulds or expectations and notice how you feel. Then reread the corresponding preference or desire and see how, if at all, your feelings change.

What did you notice?

STEP 2:
JUDGMENTS

Many of us readily judge people and situations using either-or frameworks: something is either good or bad, right or wrong, perfect or worthless. When we operate out of these rigid polarities we usually end up harshly judging and criticizing ourselves or others. The "pay-off" for this type of thinking is we either get to feel superior to others or we get a painful hit of shame and worthlessness.

Judgments and either/or thinking are closely connected to viewing people as either victims or perpetrators. I believe this mindset is a particularly dangerous trap. When I judge others as perpetrators I no longer see them in their full humanity and I can distance myself from them. Seeing myself or others as victims reinforces the illusion of helplessness and powerlessness to influence our life experiences.

> "Whenever you are about to find fault with someone, ask yourself the following question: What fault of mine most nearly resembles the one I am about to criticize?"
> — Marcus Aurelius, Meditations

There is a spiritual principle: We are what we judge. When I have criticized others in the workplace, I often realize that their behaviors reflect back and mirror something that I do not like about myself. The key is to recognize when I am being judgmental and to explore the roots and reasons I may be focusing on others in that moment.

Questions: Useful questions to explore when we notice we are judging and criticizing others include, "How am I just like this person?" and "What am I trying to avoid in me by over-focusing on them?" and "What is my "pay-off" for judging and criticizing them?"

Questions to explore when we are judging ourselves include, "What am I getting out of this self-criticism?" and "Where did I first hear this type of criticism about myself?" and "What are more reasonable, accurate assessments of the situation? Of me?

Shift Your Judgments

Directions: When we notice we are stuck in a right/wrong thinking pattern we can choose a more useful approach by identifying what is more productive or less productive given the intended outcomes of the situation. This shift away from judgments to focusing on the usefulness of actions or comments within a given context opens the possibility of exploring a wider range of solutions and approaches.

Reflect back on a difficult situation and in the left-hand column, write any judgments or right/wrong thinking that might have fueled your triggered reaction. Then rewrite these beliefs.

Judgment or right/wrong thinking	More useful thought

STEP 2:
PUTTING IT ALL TOGETHER
~ IDENTIFY YOUR
INTRAPERSONAL ROOTS

Directions: Reflect back on a difficult workplace situation where you didn't react very productively. Use the questions below to explore the possible intrapersonal roots that were restimulated at Step 2 of the Triggering Event Cycle.

1. What **current life issues and dynamics** may have been depleting your protective shield and leaving you more susceptible to feeling deeply triggered? (fatigue, burnout, illness, crises, stressors, relationship or family dynamics, problems at work, recent life transitions, death of a loved one or pet, etc.)

2. **Cumulative impact** of recent experiences: Does this situation remind you of recent events?

3. **Unresolved unfinished business and old wounds:** Does this person remind you of anyone from your past? Does this situation remind you of unhealed traumas?

4. **Fears** (check-off [☑] all that are related and add any others)

	My personal issues will become the focus of the conversation: all eyes will be on me.		If I am too confrontational or angry, then people will judge me, be mad at me, reject me, ostracize me, etc.
	I will lose credibility and be seen as less competent.		I will be seen as incompetent and "not good enough."
	If I cry and show emotion, people will think less of me....I won't be able to manage the situation.		They will see how prejudiced I really am.
	The conversation will "get out of control."		I'll let people down and disappoint them.
	People will get too emotional and I won't have the skills to manage the situation.		People won't like me or approve of me.
	I won't know enough about the issue to engage in conversation.		Things won't change.
	If I challenge this issue I will be all alone without any support.		I will make a mistake and be wrong.
	I won't be able to express myself clearly; I'll be misunderstood.		If I don't handle this well, people could feel uncomfortable...be hurt.
	People will be disappointed in me.		Things will be worse off than before.

5. **Unmet Needs/What I value*** (check-off [☑] all that are related and add any others)

Respect, dignity	
Trust	
Planning, order	
Fairness	
Clarity, understanding	
Openness, honesty	
Direct communication	
Respectful disagreement	
Recognition, acknowledgement	
Appreciation	
Competence, effectiveness	
Success, to make a difference	
Inclusion	

To be kept informed and updated	
Harmony, peace...	
Safety, security	
Integrity	
Innovation and creativity	
Ease and simplicity	
Connection	
Mutuality, partnering, collaboration	
For approval	
For acceptance, belonging	
Consideration	
Dependability, follow-through	

6. **Ego-driven desires** (check-off [☑] all that are related and add any others)

To assert, regain my power and authority	
To have control	
To win the argument; prove them wrong	
To get my way	
To make people change; "fix" them	
To make people learn	
To be right	
To shut them down, put them in their place	
To make them feel the pain and hurt I feel	
To avoid deep emotions and conflict	

To be seen as the expert, smarter than others	
To prove I am competent	
To gain prestige and status	
To be admired; avoid disgrace	
To be liked	
To fit in	
To seen as the "chosen one"	
To be perfect	
To gain certainty and predictability	
To make others engage as I want them to	
For everyone to feel happy	

7. **Biases, assumptions, expectations, shoulds, and judgments:** Which ones may have fueled your reaction?

Anticipate A Future Difficult Situation

Anticipate a triggering event you might experience in the next couple of weeks. Below, note which of these intrapersonal roots might fuel your triggered reaction in this situation.

*References:

Gill, R., Leu, L., & Morin, Judi (2009). NVC Toolkit. BookSurge Publishing.

Rosenberg, M. (2005). Nonviolent Communication: A language of life. Encinitas, CA: Puddle Dancer Press.

kathy obear
LIFE COACH
choose courage, speak your truth, live on purpose.

STEP 3:
SHIFT YOUR STORY AND CHANGE YOUR REACTION

Directions: Review the example below to understand how the story we create at Step 3 impacts the rest of The Cycle: our emotions, thoughts, and reactions.

Situation (Step 1):
When you express your concerns about the impact of a pending decision, your supervisor says, "Don't worry. That won't happen."

Step 3: **If you create this story...**	**Step 4:** **What emotions and negative** **thoughts might result?**
My supervisor is out of touch and doesn't value me or my input...	<u>Thoughts</u>: He doesn't appreciate me! Why do I invest so much of myself here? Maybe I should look for another position.... <u>Feelings</u>: Anger, resentment

Step 6: **Given your story and the resulting feelings,** **what (less productive) reaction do you initially consider/do?**
Sulking; withdrawing energetically; not participating in further conversations; I will sit back and watch as they fail

If at Step 3 you shift **your interpretation to.....**	**What emotions and thoughts** **might result at Step 4?**
My supervisor may not have all of the same data I have.	<u>Feelings</u>: Hopeful, willing to stay engaged <u>Thoughts</u>: Maybe if I share the facts I have, he will understand more of my perspective.

Step 6: Given your story and the resulting feelings, **what (more productive) reaction might you now consider?**
Offer to share some additional data and context; Ask to continue the conversation in the near future; Continue to research and gather more information

Use the same prompts to explore the impact of shifting your story at Step 3:

Situation (Step 1):
Write about a recent difficult work situation.

Step 3:
What was the story you created:

Step 4:
What were your triggered emotions?
Negative thoughts?

Feelings:

Negative thoughts:

Step 6: Given your story and the resulting feelings,
what (less productive) reactions did you initially consider?

If you shift your interpretation to...	What emotions and thoughts might result?
	Feelings: Thoughts:

Step 6: Given your revised story and the resulting feelings, what (more productive) reactions might you now consider?

STEP 4:
IDENTIFY THE FULL BREADTH OF YOUR TRIGGERED EMOTIONS

Directions: Reflect on a difficult situation where you felt deeply triggered. Review this list of feelings and circle each one that you experienced in that moment. Add any others to the list.

Aggravated	Crushed	Empowered	Impatient	Powerless
Agitated	Defeated	Empathetic	Incensed	Preoccupied
Alarmed	Deflated	Enraged	Indifferent	Puzzled
Alienated	Dejected	Envious	Indignant	Raging
Ambivalent	Depleted	Exasperated	Infuriated	Regretful
Amused	Depressed	Excited	Insecure	Relieved
Angry	Despair	Exhausted	Inspired	Remorseful
Anguish	Determined	Exhilarated	Irritated	Repulsed
Annoyed	Disappointed	Fascinated	Jealous	Resentful
Anxious	Discouraged	Fearful	Jubilant	Sad
Appreciative	Disgusted	Forlorn	Lonely	Surprised
Apprehensive	Disheartened	Frightened	Longing	Sympathetic
Appalled	Disillusioned	Furious	Mean	Tender
Awe	Dissatisfied	Grateful	Mortified	Tense
Ashamed	Distracted	Gratified	Nervous	Terrified
Bitter	Distressed	Grief	Numb	Touched
Bored	Distrustful	Guilty	Outraged	Unsettled
Burned out	Drained	Hateful	Overwhelmed	Useless
Calm	Dumbfounded	Heartbroken	Panic	Vulnerable
Carefree	Eager	Hesitant	Paralyzed	Wary
Confident	Edgy	Hopeless	Peaceful	Weary
Confused	Embarrassed	Hurt	Perplexed	Worried

What are your thoughts as you look at all your circled emotions?

Major source: Gill, R., Leu, L., & Morin, J. (2009). *NVC Toolkit*. BookSurge Publishing.

STEP 4:
IDENTIFY COMMON NEGATIVE THOUGHTS AND SELF-LIMITING BELIEFS

"It is the mind that makes the body."
Sojourner Truth

Directions: Our thoughts are like songs on a playlist that is stuck in repeat play mode. They will keep replaying over and over until we reject them and replace them with a new playlist! But we first need to recognize our old songs that may need updating. Below is a list of some common negative thoughts that people have at Step 4 about themselves, others, and the situation. Check-off (☑) any that seem familiar:

○ I can't handle this!

○ The last time this happened I just froze and fell apart

○ I am not smart enough, good enough, competent enough, creative enough...

○ I will never be able to get this done in time

○ I am such a fraud

○ I will never be able to do this

○ What I do won't make any difference

○ Things won't change

○ What do I have to offer?

○ What if I completely ruin this?

○ They will be angry when they hear about this I could make it worse

○ I have to get this right!

○ I will let people down, disappoint them

○ People could be hurt if I don't do this well

○ This could hurt my career

○ I will make a fool of myself

○ What if no one likes me

○ I won't fit in or be accepted

○ I could be all alone in this situation

○ What if I lose control?

○ This is out of control!

○ They won't understand

○ They will attack me just like last time

○ No one appreciates all I do for them

○ If I confront them, they will ostracize me

○ They are so biased and prejudiced

○ They are such @!*^#! jerks

○ They don't know what they are doing

○ This is such a waste of time just like it always is

○ I am smarter than any of them

○ They are so incompetent

○ They are all hypocrites

○ They always make things so complicated

○ This is going to be so hard and difficult

○ No one else will ever step up to do any meaningful work on this project

○ Everyone is always so difficult and unreasonable

○ She is always so rude and obnoxious

○ No one cares about what I think or feel

○ They are so self-centered

○ They'll just drop the ball again and I'll have to clean it all up as usual

○ This will be like that time everything was such a disaster

kathy obear
LIFE COACH
choose courage, speak your truth, live on purpose

STEP 4:
SELF-MANAGEMENT TOOLS
~ CHANGE YOUR
THOUGHTS

I no longer agree to treat myself with disrespect. Every time a self-critical thought comes to mind, I will forgive the Judge and follow this comment with words of praise, self-acceptance, and love.
- Miguel Ruiz

Directions: The unproductive, self-limiting thoughts we have during difficult situations decrease our effectiveness in the moment. When we change these thoughts, we are better positioned to choose effective responses. Below are some examples of how to change negative thoughts at Step 4:

When you think:	You can shift your thoughts to:
They're not getting it! This is a failure!	I will do the best I can. I am not responsible for everyone's learning. People will take away from here what they need.
I should know the answer to that!	I am not the expert here. My role is to facilitate the team's creativity. I can say, "I don't know," and ask others for their input.
You are such a *%^*#!!* for interrupting me!	I don't appreciate his timing, but at least he is willing to engage in this dialogue...He seems to have a lot of energy about this topic so maybe he has some good ideas to add...
I can't handle this!	If I make a mistake, I can use it to model that we can learn from errors and keep moving...
He is such an ignorant bigot!	I wonder why he feels so threatened? When have I felt or said something like this in the past? How can I respond to his inappropriate comment and also let him "save face?"
Her reaction is so unprofessional!	I wonder what is really going on for her. Did I say or do something that was a trigger for her?
They are so resistant!	They seem to feel safe enough to be honest about their concerns. Now we can get to the heart of this issue and maybe find a solution that meets all of our needs.
What a *@?!?# jerk!	I wonder what has happened recently that has him reacting this way?

Think about a recent difficult situation and write down several unproductive thoughts you were thinking at that time. Then identify alternative thoughts that could leave you feeling less triggered, if not more open and curious.

When you think:	You can shift your thoughts to:

STEP 4:
SELF-MANAGEMENT TOOLS
~ CALMING STATEMENTS

Directions: Read the following phrases and note which ones may be useful to help you get more grounded and centered during difficult situations.

Remind yourself about the dynamics of triggers
- I'm just triggered right now...this too shall pass...
- It's not about them, there's something going on in me...
- This could be a powerful learning moment for them, for me...

Focus on what is positive
- At least they are willing to engage in this conversation...
- A few people seem to be reflecting and more open...
- What can I learn and take away from this situation to help me in the future?

Trust the process
- Everything happens for a reason...trust the process....
- Hmm, this is curious...I wonder why this is happening right now?
- I may have over-estimated what's possible in this moment...what would be a reasonable next step from here?
- I'll just wait and see what emerges...

Adjust your approach
- She may not be willing to engage right now, but I'll bet some other folks will...
- So that approach didn't seem to work...what else can I try?
- I have responded effectively in similar situations, I can do it again.

Focus on the intent of others
- They're doing the best they can with the knowledge and resources they have...
- He's just trying to meet unmet needs...
- I trust they are not intentionally trying to undermine me...

What other thoughts would help you center yourself in difficult situations?

STEP 5:
CONSIDER THE INTENTIONS AND UNMET NEEDS OF OTHERS

Directions: In difficult situations, I can de-escalate the intensity of my emotions by considering the possible unmet needs and intentions that could be fueling the behaviors I find disruptive and ineffective. From a more grounded stance I am far more likely to respond in effective ways. I first learned of this approach through the work of Marshall Rosenberg and Nonviolent Communication.

For each of the scenarios below, imagine what might be the unmet needs fueling the person's unproductive behaviors. Some of the needs and values that seem particularly related to difficult situations I experience include dignity, respect, trust, integrity, safety, belonging, acceptance, honesty, connection, support, mutuality, partnering, community, ease, harmony, fairness, understanding, clarity, recognition, competence, effectiveness, consideration, purpose, equity, and inclusion.

Unproductive behavior	Their possible unmet needs
1. Gossiping about your to colleagues	To belong, to matter, self-expression, connection
2. Someone stays quiet and colludes with offensive behaviors	Safety, security, to belong, peace, acceptance
3. Someone is texting on their smart phone during the conversation.	
4. Someone is trying to control and micro-manage tasks	
5. Someone looks away from you as you are talking to them and asks someone else a question.	
6.	
7.	

Take a moment and focus only on the unproductive behavior:

What are your thoughts and feelings about this person?

Then, only focus on their possible unmet needs:

What are your thoughts and feelings now?

When I take the time to explore what needs someone may be trying to meet in a difficult dialogue, I gain more understanding and enough distance from them to feel less triggered and more open to engaging them in productive ways.

For further resources:

Gill, R., Leu, L., & Morin, J. (2009). *NVC toolkit*. BookSurge Publishing.

Rosenberg, M. (2005). *Nonviolent communication: A language of life*. Encinitas, CA: Puddle Dancer Press.

kathy obear
LIFE COACH
choose courage. speak your truth. live on purpose.

Step 5:
Identify Unproductive, "Negative" Intentions You Sometimes Choose

Directions: Think about a few times you have reacted less effectively during difficult conversations. As you review the following examples, check-off any of these less productive intentions that seem familiar to you, and add any additional ones (I have reacted out of all of them at some point!):

	win the argument
	get even, get them back
	to be right, prove the other person wrong
	to prove you are competent, smart
	assert your power and authority
	gain status and prestige, be admired
	be in control
	intimidate the other person
	"put them in their place"
	shut them down
	punish the other person
	embarrass or put them down
	make them feel the pain you feel
	keep the conversation "under control"
	be liked, fit in

	change the other person's views, feelings, or behaviors
	to make people learn
	trick and "outfox" the other person
	avoid intense emotions, in self and others
	make everyone feel happy and harmonious
	avoid feeling or being viewed as "incompetent"
	control how others feel about you
	ignore them
	use the current opportunity to "right the wrongs" you experienced in the past
	seek approval of others
	avoid confrontation and conflict

Next, imagine thinking some of these negative intentions. How might you react unproductively if you think these?

Step 5:
Identify the More Productive, "Positive" Intentions You Sometimes Choose

Directions: Below is a list of some of the more productive and "positive" intentions we can choose at Step 5. Check-off any that you commonly think about before you respond in difficult situations. Then star (*) those you would like to add to your "tool kit."

	engage in respectful dialogue
	create greater inclusion
	facilitate open, honest discussion
	do no harm
	leave people feeling whole
	"go with the flow," trust the process
	deepen learning and growth
	meet people "where they are" without judgment
	use the triggering moment to deepen understanding
	relate to the person, connect with them
	invite people to learn from the situation
	take time to "gather yourself"
	create space for the other person to express their feelings, perceptions
	deepen understanding across differences

	acknowledge they are doing the best they can with the resources and knowledge they have at this moment
	create safety for the expression of differing viewpoints
	encourage more people to engage in the discussion
	support people to disagree with each other in respectful ways
	model effective recovery skills when your behavior results in negative impact
	re-establish credibility with the person or group
	interrupt unproductive, inappropriate behaviors and group dynamics
	model the values you espouse: respect, authenticity, empathy, self-reflection, engagement...
	build a "bridge" and a connection with the other person
	create more effective relationships and coalitions

Next, imagine thinking some of these positive intentions. How might you respond out of these intentions?

STEP 5:
SHIFT NEGATIVE
INTENTIONS

When we choose negative intentions we are more likely to react in unproductive ways. Below is an example that shows how we can change how we respond effectively at Step 6 by shifting our intentions.

A client shared a common difficult situation they often experience on Search Committees. When the Chair asked the members for feedback on the three finalists for the position, one senior leader, Jerry said, "I like Chad. And Kelly would be fine as well. But Tiana wouldn't be a good fit. Don't get me wrong, I think diversity is important, but we also don't want to lower our standards." She was furious when no one else countered his comments. Once again she was the only one who had the courage to speak up and confront these discriminatory behaviors. Her first thought was to say something like, "This is another example of racist practices that keep our organization so lily white!" But she stopped herself knowing that this would be a CEM, a career-ending move! A couple other people offered their assessment of the candidates while she took a few deep breaths and thought through her options. She then said, "I want to ask us to slow down a moment. Before we make our recommendations, I'd like us to revisit the core competencies we identified for this position and then use these as we offer our feedback about each candidate. I actually liked all three of them on a personal level, but I think we will find some clear distinctions when we assess their demonstrated capacities against our envisioned outcomes." After a pause that seemed to last forever, the Chair agreed and they started to center the competencies in our conversation.

In the following chart I have summarized key elements of her story.

1. The less productive, "negative" intentions	3. More productive, "positive" intentions
Embarrass the colleague; call him out on his racist comment; show everyone else what they should be doing in similar situations	Address the inappropriate comment in a way that furthers learning; Refocus the conversation on competencies, away from personal opinions and "likability" of the candidates; model how to engage effectively and maintain working relationships
2. When we react less productively, what is the probable impact of our reaction?	**4. The impact when we respond out of these positive intentions**
If she had done this, she might have damaged her relationship with her colleague and other members of the committee; others wouldn't have learned how to be more effective in similar situations; She may have lost credibility in this group to influence future decisions	When she responded this way, the group members readily focused on competencies including the capacity to create inclusive work environments and effectively serve the increasingly diverse client populations; her colleague was able to "save face" and actually participated in identifying a few competencies; she believes they ended up identifying the most competent candidate for their needs

Directions: Think about a recent difficult situation in which you reacted unproductively. Make some notes in the chart that follows using the following prompts:

1. In section #1, write out 1-2 of the less productive, negative intentions you had in that moment.

2. In section #2, write how you reacted less effectively and the probable impact of your reaction.

3. In section #3, rewrite these negative intentions into more productive ones.

4. In section #4, anticipate how you MIGHT have responded more productively out of these more positive, productive intentions; and the probable impact of this response

1. The less productive, "negative" intentions

3. Rewrite into more productive, "positive" intentions

2. How did you react less productively? What was the probable impact of your reaction?

4. How might you have responded? What might be the impact from responding out of these positive intentions?

kathy obear
LIFE COACH
choose courage, speak your truth, live on purpose

STEP 6:
PAIRS ~ ADDITIONAL TOOLS TO RESPOND IN DIFFICULT SITUATIONS

A: ASK

If someone is strongly disagreeing with you, you could ask:
- Could you say more about that?
- Can you give an example?
- Can you give me some background on this situation?
- Help me understand how you came to that conclusion?
- Can you help me understand what you disagree with or find frustrating?
- Can you talk about the reasons you feel so strongly?

If you do not agree with someone's idea or opinion, you could ask:
- What are your intended outcomes for that idea?
- How does that idea advance our strategic goals?
- How does your approach connect with what I was suggesting?
- How might that play out if we go in this direction?

If you want to state your perspective after someone has disagreed with you, you can start with:
- I want to make sure I understand your point. You are saying that... How close am I in describing what you are concerned about?
- I can understand your perspective. And I'd like to share a few more thoughts....
- As I listen to you, a dilemma for me is....
- My experience has been somewhat different....
- Another way I might approach this is....
- I believe/think ____. How is this similar or different for you?

If you believe someone said something inappropriate or offensive:
- Here is what I heard you say. How well did I understand you?
- Come again? or Can you repeat that?
- What do you mean when you say...?
- Can you help me understand what you meant by that?
- What did you want to communicate with your comment?
- What message do you think that comment could send?
- Can you help me understand your intent when you said...?
- I trust you didn't intend to ____.
- You probably didn't notice what the impact of that comment was when you said...

If two or more people are in conflict and don't appear to be understanding each other's points, you could enter with:
- So, you're saying that...
- So, from your perspective...
- I want to make sure I understand your point. Are you saying that...?
- I thought I heard you say... Is that accurate?
- I may have missed some of what led up to what was said just now. Can someone help me understand the context of what is occurring?

If you sense someone hasn't fully expressed their point, you could start with:
- I'm not fully understanding your point. Can you say more?
- I'm on a learning edge here... What I'm curious about is....
- What is underneath your comment/question?
- Is there a question or a concern behind your statement?

If you sense that someone may have felt triggered by something you said, you could say:
- I'm wondering if what I said had an impact on you...
- My sense is some folks may have been impacted by what I just said...

If a colleague is upset about something but not fully discussing it, you could ask:
- Can you say more about what happened and what the impact was?
- What's the most ____ (frustrating, embarrassing, anxiety producing, etc.) part about that situation?
- What are your key concerns about this?

If you want to expand the discussion to see if others will engage the difficult dynamics, you could say:
- I am curious what others are thinking....
- What are some perspectives or reactions of others?
- How do others relate to what's been said?
- I appreciate what you're saying. Anyone have a different perspective or something else to add?

If you are concerned that you have been misunderstood, you could say:
- I want to make sure I am understood. Can you tell me what you're hearing me say?
- I'm not sure I was able to get my point across. Would you share the essence of what you heard me say?
- I believe I said something different than you heard... What I said was... Is that what you had thought?
- I'd like to clarify what I said before because it is different than what you are referencing...

If the group is struggling to move forward, you could ask:
- What do you see as the next steps?
- Are there any actions we want to avoid as we move forward?
- What would you suggest?
- One thought could be to ____. What do you think?
- Might it be possible to ____?
- I'd like us to seriously consider...

When you want a group to reflect on its processes and improve team dynamics, you could ask:
- In what ways are we working together that help us be productive?
- Are there any group dynamics that could be getting in our way?
- What might you suggest we do differently in the future?

If you want to debrief the impact of a difficult conversation with a colleague, you could ask:
- I appreciate your discussing this with me, and I'm curious how that conversation was for you?
- Is there anything you would want me to do differently in the future?
- How would you like us to discuss issues in the future?

S: SHARE

If you want to connect by sharing a story or example from your own experience, you can say:
- I can relate. Just last week, I...
- I remember when I...
- I relate. I used to...
- This reminds me of when....

If you want to share the impact of someone's comments or behavior, you can say:
- When I hear you say that, I think/feel....
- I'd like to share the impact of your comment...
- I'm feeling uncomfortable with what you're saying...
- Here's what's going on for me as I hear you....
- My concern, if we move in this direction, is...

To invite others to share their feelings or the impact they are experiencing, you can say:
- How are others reacting or impacted by this?
- I'm noticing I'm feeling____, anyone else?
- I'm noticing I have some concerns. Anyone else?
- I am deeply moved by your example. How are others impacted?
- When ____ just happened, I felt ____. Does anyone else relate to me? Or did anyone else feel triggered just now?

Self-Care:
Identify How You Spend Your Time

Directions: Use the following worksheet to begin to identify how you spend your time. Think about typical days for both the week and the weekend.

1. In the columns at the bottom of this page make a list of all the common activities you do in a day.

2. Next, use different colors to fill in the bar graphs on the following page to represent how much time you spend in each activity. Each large line on the graph represents one hour. For instance, if you sleep for eight hours, you would use one color to fill in eight spaces and then label that area "sleep." If you watch a couple of hours of TV at night, you would use a different color to fill in two space and label it "TV."

3. After you completely fill in the bar, notice how you spend your time.

4. Then, keep track of how you use your time over the next 1-2 weeks. As you review your notes, identify 2-3 changes that will help you find more time for self-care.

5. You might also want to journal each morning and evening to identify:

    *   Thoughts and activities that added value and energy to my day
    *   Thoughts and activities that left me feeling depleted

Common weekday activities: **Common weekend activities:**

WEEKDAY

WEEKEND

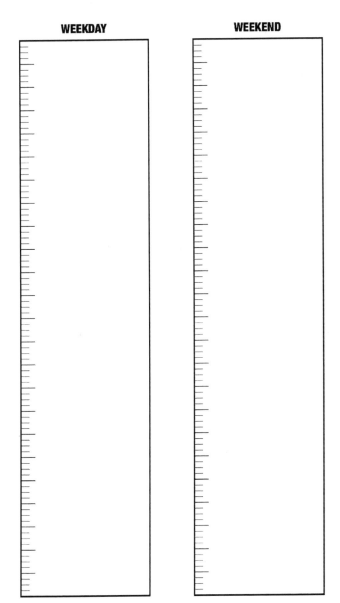

ACKNOWLEDGEMENTS

I never imagined I would be so deeply blessed with such powerful and loving mentoring and guidance over the years. Bailey Jackson supported me in my early doctoral work and helped me refine my focus on self-work and triggering events. Bob Hanna and Elsie Y. Cross were the first to challenge me and support my inner healing work at the NTL workshop, "Holding On, Letting Go." Gerry Weinstein helped me deepen my understanding of triggers and so graciously invited me to co-author a chapter that started me on my journey to share these insights and tools. Maurianne Adams was so instrumental in my completing my dissertation on this topic. Without her, I may not have finished. Her expert editing and superb insights continue to shape my thinking and writing.

I am grateful to Lisa Landreman for inviting me to write a chapter for social justice educators on navigating difficult situations and triggering events. Your patience, support, and skilled editing were invaluable to me. Writing that chapter helped me believe I could complete this book.

I have such deep gratitude for my editors, Angela Lauria and Mila Nedeljkov, and the amazing staff of The Difference Press and The Author Incubator. Your expert coaching and editing gave me the final push to birth this book. I am forever grateful.

I so appreciate the lessons, insights, and stories from all the participants in my research, the alumni of the Social Justice Training Institute as well as all the participants and clients in my training and coaching sessions. You helped me refine and deepen my understanding of triggering events and identify more strategies to navigate them effectively. And to my friends and faculty of SJTI, Jamie Washington, becky martinez, Vernon Wall, Carmen Rivera, and Sam Offer ~ I so cherish your support, love, and partnership on this journey.

Tanya Williams, I so love learning with you as we facilitate workshops on difficult conversations and triggering events. I know the participants deeply benefit from our collaborative partnership.

Pamela Graglia, thank you for your superb graphics! I so appreciate your brilliance and amazing work!

There are so many others who have supported me on this journey, far too many to name in this space ~ I hope you know how deeply grateful I am for you.

I know I was never alone in this process. I am indebted to my muses and guides for all their insights, wisdom, and loving nudges to keep writing. And most of all, to my wife and life partner, Paulette Dalpes. You have been my treasured companion on this journey. I am forever grateful for your love and support, and your belief in me for all these years. Thank you for being my greatest fan and a superb editor. I love you deeply.

ABOUT THE AUTHOR

Kathy Obear, Ed. D., has been research-ing, training, and writing about navigat-ing difficult situations for 25 years. As a trainer, consultant, speaker, and coach she has helped individuals and organi-zations rise above toxic workplace situa-tions and create more productive, inclu-sive work environments that unleash the power, passion, and creativity of every employee.

In writing this book, she has pulled from her 30 years of experience as an organizational development consultant and trainer, as well as her experiences as a Martha Beck Certified Life Coach and an Executive Coach.

If you are interested in learning more about her webinars, individual and group coaching, and training seminars for organizations, contact her at www.drkathyobear.com/contact.

Kathy lives in New York City with her wife and two amazing kitty muses!

Difference Press offers entrepreneurs, including life coaches, healers, consultants, and community leaders, a comprehensive solution to get their books written, published, and promoted. A boutique-style alternative to self-publishing, Difference Press boasts a fair and easy-to-understand profit structure, low-priced author copies, and author-friendly contract terms. Its founder, Dr. Angela Lauria, has been bringing to life the literary ventures of hundreds of authors-in-transformation since 1994.

LET'S MAKE A DIFFERENCE WITH YOUR BOOK

You've seen other people make a difference with a book. Now it's your turn. If you are ready to stop watching and start taking massive action, reach out.

"Yes, I'm ready!"

In a market where hundreds of thousands books are published every year and are never heard from again, all participants of The Author Incubator have bestsellers that are actively changing lives and making a difference.

In two years we've created over 134 bestselling books in a row, 90% from first-time authors. We do this by selecting the highest quality and highest potential applicants for our future programs.

Our program doesn't just teach you how to write a book—our team of coaches, developmental editors, copy editors, art directors, and marketing experts incubate you from book idea to published bestseller, ensuring that the book you create can actually make a difference in the world. Then we give you the training you need to use your book to make the difference you want to make in the world, or to create a business out of serving your readers. If you have life-or world-changing ideas or services, a servant's heart, and the willingness to do what it REALLY takes to make a difference in the world with your book, go to http://theauthorincubator.com/apply/ to complete an application for the program today.

Clarity Alchemy: When Success Is Your Only Option

by Ann Bolender

Cracking the Code: A Practical Guide to Getting You Hired

by Molly Mapes

Divorce to Divine: Becoming the Fabulous Person You Were Intended to Be

by Cynthia Claire

Facial Shift: Adjusting to an Altered Appearance

by Dawn Shaw

Finding Clarity: Design a Business You Love and Simplify Your Marketing

by Amanda H. Young

Flourish: Have It All Without Losing Yourself

by Dr. Rachel Talton

Marketing To Serve: The Entrepreneur's Guide to Marketing to Your Ideal Client and Making Money with Heart and Authenticity

by Cassie Parks

NEXT: How to Start a Successful Business That's Right for You and Your Family

by Caroline Greene

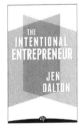

*Pain Free: How I
Released 43 Years
of Chronic Pain*

by Dottie DuParcé
(Author), John F.
Barnes (Foreword)

*Secret Bad Girl:
A Sexual Trauma
Memoir and
Resolution Guide*

by Rachael
Maddox

*Skinny: The Teen
Girl's Guide to
Making Choices,
Getting the Thin
Body You Want,
and Having the
Confidence You've
Always Dreamed Of*

by Melissa Nations

*The Aging Boomers:
Answers to Critical
Questions for You,
Your Parents and
Loved Ones*

by Frank M. Samson

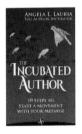

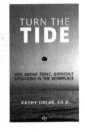

*The Incubated
Author: 10 Steps to
Start a Movement
with Your Message*

by Angela Lauria

*The Intentional
Entrepreneur: How
to Be a Noisebreaker,
Not a Noisemaker*

by Jen Dalton
(Author), Jeanine
Warisse Turner
(Foreword)

*The Paws Principle:
Front Desk
Conversion Secrets
for the Vet Industry*

by Scott Baker

*Turn the Tide:
Rise Above Toxic,
Difficult Situations
in the Workplace*

by Kathy Obear

Made in the USA
Middletown, DE
26 October 2017